Dear Sparkle

D1397613

Dear Sparkle

CAT-TO-CAT advice from the world's foremost FELINE columnist

Sparkle the Cat

Aadamsmedia
Avon, Massachusetts

Copyright © 2010 by Janiss Garza, FitCat Enterprises, Inc.
Photos © 2010 by Janiss Garza, FitCat Enterprises, Inc.
All rights reserved.
This book, or parts thereof, may not be reproduced in any
form without permission from the publisher; exceptions are
made for brief excerpts used in published reviews.

Published by
Adams Media, a division of F+W Media, Inc.
57 Littlefield Street, Avon, MA 02322. U.S.A.
www.adamsmedia.com

ISBN 10: 1-4405-0379-6
ISBN 13: 978-1-4405-0379-5
eISBN 10: 1-4405-0735-X
eISBN 13: 978-1-4405-0735-9

Printed in China.

10   9   8   7   6   5   4   3   2   1

Library of Congress Cataloging-in-Publication Data
is available from the publisher.

This publication is designed to provide accurate and authoritative information with regard to the subject matter covered. It is sold with the understanding that the publisher is not engaged in rendering legal, accounting, or other professional advice. If legal advice or other expert assistance is required, the services of a competent professional person should be sought.

—From a *Declaration of Principles* jointly adopted by a Committee of the American Bar Association and a Committee of Publishers and Associations

Many of the designations used by manufacturers and sellers to distinguish their product are claimed as trademarks. Where those designations appear in this book and Adams Media was aware of a trademark claim, the designations have been printed with initial capital letters.

Grunge picture border © istockphoto / kirstypargeter
Letter paper, page 2 © istockphoto / spxChrome
Letter paper, page 5 © istockphoto / sx70
Letter paper, page 8 © istockphoto / dowiliukas
Letter paper, page 11 © istockphoto / thumb
Letter paper, page 13 © istockphoto / chictype
Letter paper, page 16 © istockphoto / thumb

This book is available at quantity discounts for bulk purchases.
For information, please call 1-800-289-0963.

To homeless cats everywhere:
may you find humans who understand
you sufficiently so that you never have
to write me for advice.

Contents

Introduction

"A cat's got her own opinion of human beings. She don't say much, but you can tell enough to make you anxious not to hear the whole of it."

—Jerome K. Jerome

If you're a human reading this book, don't say I didn't warn you; what you are about to read is no-holds-barred advice meant for cats only. I didn't write this for you, although I will say that much of this book was written *because* of you. We cats are bright creatures, and if you share your home with one, you can undoubtedly count the many ways in which she's outwitted you. But even cats aren't infallible, and when they are stumped about a problem, they do the smart thing; they go to an expert for advice. Unfortunately, most souls who call themselves "cat experts" have one huge problem—they are *not* cats.

You humans, read this if you dare, but don't

A human cat expert will always try to solve the issue in a way that works from a human perspective, which is quite different from that of a cat's. If a cat wants to find the answer to a troubling issue, he is far better off getting advice from an authentic cat expert, i.e., another cat. For seven years, cats have been asking me for help because they know that, as a fellow feline, I'm not going to cater to some human whim, but instead offer solutions that put them first—right where they should be. The advice column on my website, *www.sparklecat.com*, has consistently been one of its most popular sections since its debut in September 2003.

But my favorite kudos have come from fellow cats. Lilly, a cat owned by book blogger Sharon Somers, put my advice to the test. "Just the other day, I knocked over my human's tea cup when she would not feed us right away. At first there was a bit of shouting, but we got our food soon after!" Another great nod came from Quasi, a fellow cat author, who wrote *The World Is Your Litter Box*. He called me "the Dear Abby of the feline world." I know enough about human advice columnists to realize that you can't get higher praise than that!

expect to like a lot of what I have to say.

All this brings me to this book, in which I address all possible kitty conundrums! I wish I could say that cats' problems have decreased since I began my column. But, no. Whenever I think I've seen every food or litter box issue ever created, a new one comes along to surprise me. But I don't mind. It keeps me on my toes (which is how I walk normally anyhow). In addition to advice, I have also sprinkled some "Sparkle Says" tips throughout the book—these are extra tidbits of information that cats will enjoy.

A cat is never at anyone's service. The same does not apply to my advice, however, and I hope it serves my fellow cats well. You humans, read it if you dare, but don't expect to like a lot of what I have to say. If you keep an open mind, however, who knows? You just may learn something. I hear you guys are teachable when you want to be.

Sparkle 🐾
Los Angeles, California

Games Kitties Play

We cats can make a toy out of just about any inanimate (or animate) object. Twist-ties, pens, antique porcelain, crickets—everything's fair game. There's nothing more joyful than galloping through a dark house at three A.M.! Unfortunately, not every species has such a well-developed play instinct. Humans, for example—their sense of play is almost as dull as their sense of smell. So it's no surprise that many cats write me, complaining that they're not being allowed their full measure of fun. Such letters always sadden me. Kitties thrive on play, and a lack of recreation can lead us to act out. But then, some humans consider many of our amusements inappropriate to begin with. So you can see why this topic alone keeps me *very* busy doling out advice.

Boredom Busting

Dear Sparkle,

My human must be a member of the *inhu-mane* society! She gets up, dumps food in a dish, and then leaves for the day—and sometimes most of the evening too! The long days are the worst, because when she gets back, she's usually in a foul mood. Meanwhile, I'm alone with nothing to do and no toys, so I have to make up games from scratch. Unfortunately, my human hates my games, even though she isn't even around when I'm playing. For a while I was racing up the curtains—it's a great combo of muscle building and cardio, as you know. But when my human saw all the claw marks in the curtains, she started scream-ing, "Bad kitty!" Then I thought it might be fun to dig the plants out of their pots. She has them all over the house, so I figured this would keep me busy for a long time. She hated that too. I'm at my wit's end. Is there a way I can make my human stop blowing up at my attempts to entertain myself? Or better yet, just stay home and play with me herself?

Signed,

Going Loco

It's not your job to make
your human happy.

Dear Loco,

As much as you would like your human to change her schedule so that it revolves around you (which, of course, is every kitty's dream), it's not going to happen. If your human was smart (few are), she would find ways to keep you entertained while she is out doing unpleasant things that make her come home grouchy. She could put bird feeders outside a window where you could perch and watch. Or fill your home with cat toys that suit your personality. Since you like climbing curtains and digging in pots, I would recommend a cat tree at least five feet tall and a wooden box with holes in it, so you could reach in and grab the toys and treats inside. But if your human is too clueless to bring home some toys, try some fun activities that won't make her as mad as your curtain climbing game. Maybe bat some pens under the couch and play with them until they're totally out of reach. Or perhaps you could play hockey in the bathtub with the cap from a shampoo bottle. Could you race around the house without breaking anything that your human treasures *too* highly? You'll know what works and what doesn't by your human's reaction when she finally comes home. While it's not your job to make your human happy (and never let her tell you any differently), it's always best to keep some semblance of peace in your home. 🐾

Mayhem After Midnight

Dear Sparkle,

My humans' schedule stinks! They always sleep during the best time to play, which is around three A.M. I do my best to wake them up—I pounce on them, run through the house, knock things off their nightstand, you know, the usual—but it never works. They just get mad and yell at me. I don't understand why they are such lame-os. If I did the same to any cat, he'd be up in an instant and ready to rumble! It seems that all my humans want to do is roll over and go back to sleep. Is this because they're old? I am three and a half and they have to be at *least* ten times my age. I just thought that maybe humans age slower than cats, since they live so much longer. In any case, how can I get these humans to wake up and play?

Signed,

Frisky

You can't expect
your humans to
behave like cats.

Dear Frisky,

You can't expect your humans to behave like cats. It just isn't possible. Humans are not as tuned in to the world as cats are. They can't drop down and nap at will. Their lumbering bodies are *anything* but agile. They place excessive importance on useless things like sitting in front of a desk and fiddling around with strange, uninteresting machines. Do you really expect such dull, graceless creatures to understand that four A.M. is playtime? I hate to bum you out, but it has nothing to do with age—it's human nature! What you really need is a friend who understands the important things in life, whose schedule more closely resembles your own. I am referring, of course, to another cat. If you had a roommate to pal around with, you wouldn't feel the need to get your humans up at what they consider an "ungodly hour." Of course, this will probably still happen since you and your friend will *both* be jumping on the bed, knocking things off the nightstand, and tearing through the house. But of course, that's not *your* problem, and this advice column is for cats, not humans. 🐾

Getting a Leg Up

Dear Sparkle,

When I was a kitty, I was adopted by a human who was really great. We'd play lots of silly games, like "attack the hand," and he even taught me how to fetch my fuzzy ball. But my favorite game was at mealtime—he'd open my can of food, and I'd climb up his leg, and keep going until I reached his shoulder. Well, I've been here a year and a half now, and for some reason he doesn't like that game anymore! Whenever I try, he starts yelling and a few times, when I accidentally scratched through his pants or shirt, he got really angry. What's up with that? Doesn't he like me anymore?

Signed,

PLAYFUL BUT PUZZLED

Sparkle Says

If you are a cat over one year of age, you are not a "little baby." Feel free to inform your humans of this.

Dear Playful,

This may not have occurred to you, but now that you are a full-grown cat, you weigh much more than you did as a kitten. What was cute coming from a seven-ounce kitty with baby claws could actually do significant damage when done by a fifteen-pound cat with big-kitty claws. While I agree your human is something of a spoilsport, I have to admit that you are probably hurting him when you climb up his leg, and destroying his wardrobe besides. It's true, petty concerns like clothing mean nothing to cats, but look at it this way: the more humans spend on clothing, the less they have to spend on their cats. So it's in your best interest to retire your human-climbing game completely.

In all fairness, I think your human should take a large part of the blame for this unfortunate situation. He should have been thinking ahead to the day when your game wouldn't be so fun anymore and gently discouraged it from the start. That's one problem a lot of humans have—they don't think things through and then they are unhappy with the outcome. As cats, it's not our job to anticipate problems. That is what humans are for!

As cats, it's not our job to anticipate problems.

Game Off

Dear Sparkle,

I am a nine-month-old kitten with a fun
new game! But—of course—my humans don't
like it. They have this big screen that
they like to sit and watch for hours on
end, which is on top of this big wooden
box. The screen isn't all that interest-
ing, but what's behind the wooden box
is. There are loads of stringy things to
play with and pull! A couple of times
I pulled one of these strings too hard
and the screen went blank. Boy, was the
male human furious about that! He started
yelling that he was missing "the game"
and told me to leave. The female human
wasn't happy either because she said that
playing with strings is dangerous. Huh?
What's this game that the male human
loves so much, and how can it be dangerous to pull on a silly little string?

Signed,

String Fling

Dear Fling,

I have to side with your female human in this case—the strings you have been enjoying so much really *are* dangerous and you shouldn't be playing with them. They're called electrical cords, and if you bit into one, or stuck your claw in the socket it's plugged into, you could get zapped! This is very serious stuff—but leave it to a male human to be more concerned about his "game." Let me try to explain it in kitten terms. You know how much fun it is to chase a fuzzy ball, right? Well, imagine two cats chasing one ball. A human game is kind of like that, except instead of two humans chasing a ball, it's a whole bunch of them. I guess that might be fun if you like a crowd, but most humans who enjoy these games don't even *play* them. They sit in front of that screen and watch other humans chase the ball! If I saw a ball moving on a screen, I'd want to chase it, but humans never do that. They just yell at the screen. It's yet another curious human habit that is beyond feline comprehension. In any case, you should leave the male human to his "game" and stop playing with those electrical cords. If he were smart, he'd take some time away from that screen, wrap up those "strings," and hide them away so they aren't so tempting to you. 🐾

Garbage Games

Dear Sparkle,

We've got killer toys at my house! Q-tips, twist-ties, and those plastic rings from the milk jugs my human brings home. I play with them constantly; sometimes I'll pull all-nighters to play! I even talk to them sometimes, although I admit that's an odd habit. I really, really love my toys, but every time my human finds me playing with one of my favorites, she takes it away! Even worse, she puts it in the trash. She thinks my toys are junk! I keep losing all my best possessions this way and I'm starting to get a complex.

Signed,

Treasure or Trash?

Go right into the trash and retrieve your possessions!

Dear TOT,

Your human should be grateful you love to play with Q-tips and twist-ties—it means that she doesn't have to spend her beloved money on cat toys, which are usually second-rate anyhow. Who wants lame store-bought catnip mice or jingly plastic balls that lumber along the floor, instead of skittering the way a good milk jug ring will? Let's not even get into those elaborate mechanical toys that require batteries to work (humans always forget to buy the batteries). The higher the price tag, the more useless they generally are. Whether your human has tried replacing your good toys with store bought, or she hasn't even bothered getting you new ones, it really doesn't matter. It's criminal to deprive you of your fun, and I think it's about time you take the law into your own hands: go right into the trash and retrieve your possessions! The good thing is that many times, a trashcan will reveal additional treasures, such as tuna and cat food cans that still contain juice, greasy butter wrappers, and other items of value that humans carelessly throw away. Granted, your human will not be pleased to have you rummaging through the trash, so do it when she's not around. But really, she should have thought of that before she began treating your belongings like they were garbage. 🐾

Playtime Time Out

Dear Sparkle,

My human doesn't play with me enough!
I mean, she'll play with me at least once a
day, sometimes more, but she cuts our playtime way short. Like if that phone thing
starts ringing and she begins talking into
it, all bets are off. And she'll also quit
for really dumb reasons, like being "tired"
or because she has "errands" to run. Obviously, none of this is anywhere nearly as
important as playing with me. I never knew
humans got bored and distracted so easily!
How do I get mine to spend more time on
important stuff (ahem, playing), and less
time goofing off?

Signed,

Playgrrl

Sparkle Says

There are no
bad cats, just
poorly trained
humans.

Are you playing
with a consistent
amount of enthusiasm?

Dear Playgrrl,

Humans *are* hard to train—which means you have to be a good trainer. And a human like yours, who has the attention span of a gnat, requires you to be especially persistent. But before you point your paw, examine your own training style. Are you playing with a consistent amount of enthusiasm, or do you slack off—looking out the window when you should be chasing a crinkly ball, or stopping to take a bath instead of leaping after the feather toy? If your human thinks you are losing interest, she'll be quick to put the toys away and go do whatever else she considers "important." Humans perform best when they are rewarded, and when it comes to playing with their cats, the reward is seeing how excited we are and how much fun we are having. You can't just take a break and wander off, or you will lose her attention.

If your human insists on halting a lively play session to do something boring, run in front of her and block the doorway to keep her from leaving. You might think this looks desperate, but it's not, if you have the right attitude. You're not begging here. You are demanding she stop her foolishness and get back to the important task of keeping you happy. One of the most important aspects of training your human is making sure she has her priorities straight. 🐾

Wet and Wild

Dear Sparkle,

We are a pair of young girl cats who found a new home after a brief stay at a cat rescue. We've been here for two months and have come to the conclusion that our human is very strange! She gives us a big bowl of water, and then gets upset when we splash around in it! We bat at the water with our paws, wrestle a bit and inevitably, the bowl gets knocked over. But our human thinks we're supposed to *drink* the water! She's always mopping up the water and moaning about her floor. Once she tried getting us a bowl with running water—that was scary! In any case, we think drinking the water is a waste of a good time! How can we calm down our uptight human?

Signed,

Water Babies

Your human will go out
   of her way to accommodate
your odd habits.

Dear Water Babies,

You may think your human is strange, but I think you both are a little weird too. I am not a fan of water sports, or anything that risks my getting wet. Most cats are like me, but there does seem to be a water-loving minority. I wonder if you all are related. Anyhow, I understand that your home is still new to you, and you want to avoid upsetting your human, but you know what? You really don't have to. Give it a few more weeks and you'll discover that your human—if she's worthy of having you live with her—will go out of her way to accommodate any odd habits you may have. At first she may try to make you do things her way (i.e., the water fountain). But you needn't modify your behavior one bit. Eventually your human will realize she's the only one who cares whether her floor gets ruined, and she'll go out and get some sort of absorbent mat to put underneath your water bowl. And that'll be the end of it. 🐾

On a Roll

Dear Sparkle,

I just discovered the funnest game ever!
Next to the human litter box is this
soft bunch of paper on a roll. When
I paw on it, it comes unwound and flies
all over the place! You have no idea how
great this is! One night while my humans
were out, I unwound all the paper rolls
in the whole house! This was no easy
task since there are four human litter
boxes here—two upstairs and two down-
stairs! I thought my humans would be
glad to see that I found a way to amuse
myself, since they never give me any
of my own toys to play with, but they
were not happy at all! They said I made
a mess and that I misbehaved! Now they
shut the doors to the human litter boxes
and I can't get in to play! My humans
are fun killers! I need to get back to
my game!

Signed,

Paper Pusher

Get your fun in before
you get caught.

Dear Paper Pusher,

Shame on your humans for not getting you any toys—and then scolding you for trying to make your own fun. When your humans came home to find four rooms full of shredded paper, they got exactly what they deserved! Smart humans would get the hint and immediately go to the pet store and buy you a bunch of toys and perhaps a cat tree or two. Instead, they shut the door to your one source of entertainment. This will not do. With a little bit of kitty ingenuity, you should be able to get through those closed doors. If their doorknobs are long levers, you can grab them and pull down and they will open right up for you. Even if the doorknobs are the round variety, you still have a chance—sometimes a door doesn't latch right, or a human forgets to shut it all the way. Then it's a simple matter of pushing against it with all your weight. The door should open without too much effort. Check the doors frequently—eventually a human will forget and leave one open. Once you can get in, go right for the paper roll and have at it! Get your fun in before you get caught. One more tip: there *are* more paper rolls in the kitchen. The paper is thicker and don't unroll as quickly, but if you leap on the counter and start tearing one to shreds, it's a good way to send a message to your clueless humans. 🐾

Cat Tree Tragedy

Dear Sparkle,

A couple of years ago my humans got me the coolest cat tree ever! It was even taller than the guy human, had a bunch of places for me to sit, and not one but *two* cozy, carpeted napping tubes! Oooooh, how I've loved this cat tree ever since my humans brought it home, and I've spent every single day on it, sleeping, playing, stretching, and scratching it all over. I consider it my second home. But now disaster has struck: my humans are trying to replace it! They are calling my beloved tree "old" and "ratty," and yesterday they brought home a new one! The new one is about the same size as the one I already have, only it has little houses instead of tubes and two posts instead of one. But I don't care! I like my OLD tree, and the new one smells gross, like chemicals or something. Luckily, my humans haven't thrown out my cat tree yet. Actually, they can't because I'm on strike and won't come down from it! How can I get them to send back the new tree?

Signed,

Tree Hugger

All those rips, tears, and cat fur
mark this tree as yours.

Dear Tree Hugger,

You see your old cat tree as comfortably broken in, while your humans view it as a ragged old eyesore. But you shouldn't reject the new cat tree so quickly, since it sounds like it's got a lot of great features—the little houses for napping, two sisal posts, etc. You've had your old tree for so long that you probably don't remember that it, too, smelled funny when it first came home from the store. Once you've scratched the new one all over and rubbed up against every inch of it, it'll start smelling like a real cat tree. So keep an open mind and in the meantime, see if you can get your humans to keep the old cat tree too. Humans are very visual creatures and they are very particular, which explains why they have such a bad attitude about your tree. If it were one of their pieces of furniture, like a bed or a chair, they would probably get rid of it without a second thought. They don't realize that in your world, all those rips, tears, and permanently embedded cat fur mark this tree as yours and yours alone. If they finally get the idea that you really love this tree (and the way you are hanging onto it, it should be obvious), maybe they will keep it, and just put it somewhere where visiting humans won't see it. Now, that would be an ideal situation—two cat trees are definitely better than one! 🐾

Barrette Breakaway

Dear Sparkle,

My weird human keeps buying cat toys—for herself! What's even stranger is that instead of playing with them, she puts them in her hair. I really don't get this oddball behavior, but I'm psyched about all the cat toys. As soon as she takes them out of her hair, I knock them off the bathroom counter, pick them up with my claws and toss them into the bathtub. Those little metal things make for a great hockey game! The first few times I did this, my human laughed and said it was cute, but after I lost a couple of them, she began hiding them from me. What gives? I mean, they're obviously cat toys, *not human toys* and she isn't really playing with them anyhow, just clipping them in her hair. I want my toys back.

Signed,

Hockey Enthusiast

Sparkle Says

A celebrity cat doesn't walk down the red carpet. She sharpens her claws on it.

Dear Hockey Enthusiast,

Fortunately, humans aren't very good at hiding things from cats, so you should be able to find your toys (which your human calls barrettes) without much trouble. The first place to look is the drawers in the bathroom. They should be easy to open. It's just a matter of snagging a claw in the lip and pulling. If they don't budge, use more than one claw, or use both paws. You may have to open every drawer to find them, but be persistent. Once you find your toys, pull all of them out and have yourself one big hockey blowout! If you have a good-natured human, she will be impressed with your industriousness; if she is a bit short-tempered, she might not find your antics so amusing. I would suggest you plan for the latter event and make sure to keep a few of these metal cat toys for yourself. Hide them somewhere your human isn't likely to look—under the sofa, behind some books on a shelf, or some other small, dark place. Just remember where you put them—you don't want to lose them again! One note: this is all fine for the metal and plastic toys that humans call barrettes and hair clips. If they are stretchy and rubbery, I recommend you stay away from them. If you eat them, you could get a stomachache, or worse. If your human was hiding rubbery toys from you, she had your best interests in mind.

Yarn Spinner

Dear Sparkle,

I feel sorry for my human. She keeps coming home with these fluffy balls of yarn, but she doesn't know how to play with them. She uses these metal hooks—I assume because she doesn't have claws—and tries to grab at them, but all she ever does is tie them in big, clumsy bunches of knots! How sad is that? So I try to show her the right way to do it—tossing a ball in the air, unwinding it, and covering the floor with long, twisted strands—but she gets mad! I guess she thinks I am trying to show off, but really, I'm not. In fact, I'd love nothing more than to have her join in the fun. How can I teach her the joys of yarn play?

Signed,

Wild 'n' Wooly

There's not much you can do about your human's warped version of yarn play.

Dear Wooly,

It may not look that way to you, but your human actually thinks she *is* playing with those balls of yarn. Humans think yarn play is taking those long strands, knotting them up with those metal hooks and making stuff out of them, usually things to wear. They call it "crocheting." Yes, this is totally backwards—as cats, we know that play means to *destroy* things, not *create* them—but humans do nearly everything backwards, and we spend a lot of our time undoing all their mistakes. However, there's not much you can do about your human's warped version of yarn play. Once she has the strands knotted up, they are almost impossible to undo. You could chew through a strand or two of one knotted-up piece and that might cause the rest of it to unravel, but it takes more effort than is worthwhile. And you can take the unknotted yarn and toss it and spread it around as much as you want, but it's never going to inspire your human to do it along with you. This is one area where humans are just plain unteachable. When it comes to properly enjoying balls of yarn, you are on your own, so you might as well hide away a few of your favorites and keep them to yourself. I'm sure your human won't miss them, and if she does, she can always go out and buy more. 🐾

Strange Invasions

A cat's home is not her castle—it's her whole universe, especially if she's indoors-only, like I am. So you can imagine how aggrieved we are when some strange creature comes along and squats on our property. There are only two types of beings we accept on our turf without complaint: those that give us food and those that *are* food. Not in either category? Then who needs you? Considering how famous we cats are for protecting our territory, and marking it if necessary, I'm constantly amazed at the ways we cats get our space invaded. You will be too when you read these yowls for help.

Gauche Guest

Dear Sparkle,

I swear our house has a revolving door.
My human is one of those annoying people
who always has guests come over and visit.
I refuse to be intimidated by these tres-
passers, however, and always make my presence—and my dominance—known. But I'm having
a problem with this one woman. She calls
herself, "a bona-fide crazy cat lady," but
really, she is just plain crazy. We're
talking insane. She won't leave me alone!
She claims that all cats adore her (which
I'm sure is a bold-faced lie), and she
always tries to grab me and touch me. Even
worse, she has this awful, fake-flowery
smell and if she does manage to get her
grimy paws on me, I smell like her for
the rest of the day. Even after a thorough
wash, that floral stench sticks with me! Is
there some way I can make her stop manhan-
dling me without having to leave the room
completely? I want to show her who's boss.

Signed,

Miffed Meower

You rule your household
with a quiet, but firm paw.

Dear Miffed,

Oh no, you've encountered one of those horrible people called "cat groupies." They aren't real cat people because they don't know the first thing about how to behave around cats. They force themselves on us and talk to us like we're idiots. A REAL cat person wouldn't dream of laying a hand on us until we've checked them out and given them the go-ahead. The only thing worse than being pawed and manhandled by a cat groupie is being pawed and manhandled by one who is wearing that offensive human accessory called "perfume." While hiding under the sofa or leaving the room completely would keep you away from her, I agree—you must show her your dominance and teach her to stop messing with you. It sounds like you rule your household with a quiet, but firm paw. However, when this woman comes over, you will have to change your tactic and become the feral kitty from hell. If she won't respect your space, feel free to disrespect hers by growling and hissing at her whenever she comes near you. If she manages to grab you, struggle and break free—and tear her clothing with your claws as much as possible while you're doing it. She will eventually give up with the remark, "Well, *most* cats like me," and she will probably think there's something wrong with you. But who cares? Anyone who really knows you already knows the truth. 🐾

Reptile Rendezvous

Dear Sparkle,

The most exciting thing happened a couple of weeks ago—a lizard got in the house! Even better, it's *still* in the house! It's like having a game at my paw tips 24-7. Every time I wake up from a nap, I go hunting for it. I never know where I might find it—under the stove, behind the bookcase, scrambling up the headboard in the bedroom—that thing could be anywhere. The only thing is my humans think I've gone mad. In fact, it's worse than that. They think I'm senile because I spend so much time staring at the space behind the kitchen cabinet, or looking under the sofa. Admittedly, at twelve I am no spring kitten, but I'm not ancient, either. My eyes, nose, hearing, and mind are fine and they are all telling me there's a lizard in the house that must be chased! How can I convince my humans I haven't lost my mind?

Signed,

Lizard Lover

Sparkle Says

We cats are sleek, divinely crafted killing machines. Never let your humans forget this. A carefully placed dead cricket that's missing a leg or two is generally sufficient.

There's nothing more
fun than a prolonged
hunting session.

Dear Lizard Lover,

There's something I find far more curious than your humans' thoughts on your sanity (because who really cares what they think, anyway?): how come this lizard has been in your home for two weeks and it's still alive? It's true that there's nothing more fun than a prolonged hunting session, but that means tossing your prey around for a few minutes, not stalking it for days on end. Frankly, if this creature's been running around free all this time and you haven't killed it yet, it leaves me wondering about either your hunting skills or your mental skills. So I may actually side with your humans on this. If you think I am off the mark, then prove me wrong and stop dilly-dallying. Catch this lizard once and for all. That's the one thing that will prove to your humans (and me) that you have all your faculties. If you plop a dead lizard down at their feet, they'll know that your staring into strange places had a purpose all along. In fact, you don't even have to capture the lizard completely—just pull its tail off and present it to your humans. And make sure you do so at a moment when you are sure to have their complete attention, such as when they're eating dinner or entertaining guests. If you're going to prove that you're as sharp and spry as ever, you want to have as many witnesses as possible. 🐾

Pet Sitter Protest

Dear Sparkle,

Every time my humans leave town, they have this strange woman come over to feed us and spend the night. She's called a "pet sitter," and my three roommates (two tabbies from the local rescue, and the fuzzy gray cat who showed up at the back door one day) tell me she's cool, but I don't believe them. She smells funky and even the food smells different when she gives it to us. Whenever this strange woman comes over, I hide under the bed until my humans return. Now they are pulling out those dreaded suitcases again, which means that pet sitter is coming back. Is there some way to get her out of the house so I can have some peace, or is it true, like my roommates say, that I can use her to my advantage?

Signed,

Dubious

Show her who
rules your home.

Dear Dubious,

It's true that pet sitters can be manipulated, just like any other human, but not as much as your roommates may believe. Before your humans leave home, they give the pet sitter a bunch of rules that they must follow. So if you're an overweight cat who thinks you might weasel an extra treat or two out of the pet sitter, you're out of luck. She has already been warned not to give you any. And she probably won't offer you any out-of-the-ordinary food or treats, no matter how yummy, because they might not agree with you. Even worse, if the vet has prescribed you any medication, you will still have to take it. On the other hand, if you like to play, you can probably get her to pull out your favorite toys. Her job is to keep you happy, so it's likely she will play with you for longer periods of time than your humans do. And—surprise!—I bet she will also keep your litter box cleaner too.

So, pet sitters are a mixed bag. If you are expecting special food or if you are sick, you're not going to enjoy her very much. But she might treat you even better than your humans do. So hold your nose and give her a chance. If you decide you still don't like her, you can always annoy her by wrestling on the bed with your roommates all night. That should at least show her who rules your home. 🐾

Copied Cat

Dear Sparkle,

I'm so mad I could spit! My human keeps
on bringing home different cats and claim-
ing it's the same one. True, they all do
look alike—tuxedo cats with a distinc-
tive white spot around one eye—but it's
not the same cat because they never smell
alike. The only thing that *is* the same is
the story. I make friends with the cat,
and then my human says she is taking him to
the vet. The cat disappears for a few days,
and then my human shows up with the impos-
tor. So I do what's only natural—I attack
the interloper for invading my space without a proper introduction. My human then
separates us and I calm down and the cat
doesn't smell so weird any more. It's bad
enough that a traumatic incident like that
happens once, but over the past few years,
this has happened *three times*! The stupidest part is my human acts like it's always
the same cat. Her nose must be out of whack
because it's so obvious that it's not! Is
my human trying to make a fool out of me,
or is she the one who is being fooled?

Signed,

FERAL OVER FAUX FRIENDS

It's not a cat switcheroo
that's going on,
it's a smell switcheroo.

Dear FOFF,

It's not that your human is being played the fool, but rather she *is* a fool for not realizing what is going on every time she takes the tuxedo cat to the vet. It's not a cat switcheroo that's going on, it's a *smell* switcheroo, which really is almost as bad. When cats go to the vet, especially if they have to stay overnight or go under anesthesia, they come back smelling like completely different kitties. And as you know, we cats rely on our sense of smell even more than we do on our eyes. Our eyes may trick us, but our noses rarely do—except when a trip to the vet is involved. So while it really *is* the same cat that comes home every time, he might as well be a stranger because he smells like one. Your human doesn't get this because humans don't use their scent mechanisms to identify their friends and family. They look for familiar visuals and mannerisms instead. Too bad your human can't douse him with *eau de old cat* before she brings him home, or at the very least rub catnip all over the two of you so you both smell like something pleasant. If your roomie goes away for a day or two again, I suggest you make yourself scarce until he gets his smell back and loses that offensive vet odor. Since your human's nose—and brain—function at such a low level, it's about all you can do. 🐾

Kitten Craziness

Dear Sparkle,

I am seventeen years old, and I expected to have some peace in my senior years. Well, that wish went out the window a few months ago, when my human brought home a ten-week-old kitten. He was a cute little thing—still is—and I don't dislike him, but he is also a bundle of perpetual motion! And, unfortunately, all his activity is directed at me. I'll be dozing in my favorite sunny spot and next thing I know, I'm being attacked! Or I'll just be walking down the hallway, minding my own business and he comes leaping out at me from behind a doorway. When he's not behaving like a monster, he's actually a nice kitten and I'd rather not apply corporal punishment. Is there some other way to make him stop?

Signed,

Exasperated Elder

You may have to
distract this
kitten yourself.

Dear Exasperated,

You're very kind-hearted—most cats would have slapped that hyperactive kitten into submission long ago. Of course, it's not the kitten's fault that he has become such an annoyance in your life. He's probably under-stimulated—in other words, I bet your human doesn't have any toys for him, or she has the wrong toys, or she doesn't spend enough time playing with him herself. Judging from your age, it has probably been a while since there were kittens around, so your human has probably forgotten what a handful they are. Besides that, many humans have a low play instinct—it's really rather pathetic. It seems to get drained out of them somewhere on the way to adulthood. So you may have to distract this kitten yourself. Kittens will play with almost anything, so maybe you can knock some pens off a table for him to chase, or grab some barrettes from the bathroom countertop, or clothespins from the laundry room. You might also show him the joys of gnawing on books and magazines, or encourage him to play on top of the curtains. Once he's busy with any of these activities, you'll have a chance to get some needed rest. Your human might become upset when she finds her pens missing or her curtains shredded, but she has only herself to blame for not coming up with recreational activity for the little guy herself. 🐾

Rescue Roadhouse

Dear Sparkle,

When my human first brought me home from the rescue place, I was her only cat, and that was just fine by me. But for the past six months there has been some really crazy stuff going on! My human keeps bringing home strange cats, but they never stick around. It always starts the same way—she shows up with a cat carrier and sticks the latest cat in a room all by itself for a few days. Then after a while, the cat is usually let out to wander around the rest of the house. Sometimes they are okay and sometimes I don't like them. If there's a cat I especially dislike (that really annoying tortie who was briefly here, for example), my human sticks it back in the room by itself—I'll give her that much. But then, just as I'm getting used to having the cat around, she takes it away! I am not thrilled with this at all. My human has turned my happy home into a roadhouse! What is going on?

Signed,

Extremely Annoyed

All these cats passing
through disrupts your
peaceful routine.

Dear Annoyed,

I think I know what your human's curious behavior is about. I bet she's bringing home cats from that rescue place where she found you and is "fostering" them! Basically that means that she's keeping them at your home temporarily because either 1) they've run out of room at the rescue, 2) they have "issues" and need to adapt to being around humans, or 3) they have the kind of personalities that do better in a home than at a rescue with a bunch of other cats. I wouldn't be surprised if you started off as a foster cat yourself (I'll bet that never occurred to you!). While it's very nice and generous of your human to do this for these kitties, I do have to agree that it's really annoying to have all these cats passing through. It disrupts your peaceful routine. I can only conclude, however, that it doesn't annoy you all that much, otherwise you would have made your displeasure clear by either rejecting your litter box or beating up the other cats. And if you had done that, your human probably wouldn't keep bringing all those strange cats home. So I'm not really sure what your problem is. Maybe you're just one of those cats who likes to complain. If you are, then I suggest you complain to your human. She's the one who can do something about the situation, not me. 🐾

Housekeeper Havoc

Dear Sparkle,

Usually things are nice and quiet around my house, but every few days this horrible woman comes over and creates havoc. She moves things around and makes everything smell awful. That's bad enough, but then she pulls out this monstrous contraption that roars and sucks up everything in its path. It's all I can do to run outside until it goes away. Can you please tell me how to get this woman and her monster machine out of my life?

Signed,

Scared for My Life

Sparkle Says

Kitty Tip #78: Crinkly paper noises really annoy humans. You know that already, but the real trick is doing it repeatedly for added emphasis.

It probably isn't dangerous, as long as you stay out of its path.

Dear Scared,

You might be overreacting about the machine. If you examined it from a safe distance (under the couch or a bed is always good), you would see that it moves far more slowly than a cat and it's rather clumsy. Plus, it won't even move unless there's a human pushing it, so it is also lazy. It probably isn't dangerous, as long as you stay out of its path. Here's a rule to go by: if you are far enough away so that the noise doesn't hurt your ears, you are probably safe.

I would be more concerned about that weird smelling stuff that woman puts all over everything. Humans have this odd habit of putting smelly potions on surfaces. They call it "cleaning." Shows how stupid they are. A little dirt never hurt anything, but those potions are often toxic. Many commercial cleaning solutions can make us sick, especially anything containing phenol, which is often found in the pine-scented stuff. Even dryer sheets aren't good for us to be around, and mothballs can kill us cats. So stay away from that bad-smelling stuff, always. Some thoughtful humans only use old-fashioned, natural cleaning solutions like non-chlorine bleach, vinegar, and baking soda. Hopefully the smelly stuff this woman is using is safe for you, but as far as getting rid of her, I'm sorry to say I don't have any suggestions. Most of my ideas only wind up making situations that create a need for these people. 🐾

Takeover Makeover

Dear Sparkle,

Lucky me, I have two homes and two sets of humans. I found the second family through a cat I made friends with—they're actually *his* humans. I am glad he befriended me. My other family has a bunch of other cats and they all hate me. The new humans are a lot of fun, especially the guy. He plays with me until I'm exhausted and we take naps together sometimes. I enjoy my newer humans so much that I spend most of my days at their house. The only problem is that the cat that brought me there in the first place is mad at me now! He gets grouchy whenever I play with his (our) humans and he won't even let me sleep on the bed anymore. I guess he must be jealous, but I really want to keep his friendship. What can I do?

Signed,

Convivial Kitty

Lay back and let your friend set the pace.

Dear Convivial,

You play innocent, but I know your type. You're The Cat Who Takes Over. Your friend brings you home and introduces you to his family, then next thing he knows, you've commandeered his humans. I'm not surprised he's at his wit's end. And I have a sneaking suspicion that the other cats in your first family have had issues with you for similar reasons. Cats like you are often better off as only kitties, but unfortunately you've wound up with not one, but two multi-cat families (or rather, the second one was an only-cat family until *you* came along). Right now you are disrupting them both, so pick just one place to call home. If you choose the second home, acknowledge that it's an honor for your friend to share his humans with you instead of thoughtlessly taking up all their time (his humans are at fault for encouraging your imposition). So lay back and let your friend set the pace. If he doesn't want you on the bed, you will just have to stay off it until he gives you the go-ahead. We cats are famously lousy at such concepts as "compromise" and "give and take," but if you really want to be a member of a happy home, you've got to stop behaving as if you're the only cat that matters. Take this wise lesson from successful feral cat colonies: feline opportunism must always be tempered with the understanding of your place in the hierarchy. 🐾

The Un-Kitty

Dear Sparkle,

I am a female Siamese and I pride myself on my beauty and my royal bloodline. So you can imagine how I felt when my human came home with the oddest-looking, ugliest cat I've ever seen. It has floppy, deformed ears and there must be something wrong with it because most of the time it is left in a cage and kept in solitary confinement. I've tried to get a closer look at it, but whenever I come near, it starts getting violent and stomping its feet. This weird cat seems to be a very dangerous creature. Why in the world would my human want it? It gives me the creeps. What's the best way to convince my human that it must go?

Signed,

REPULSED IN RIVERSIDE

Sparkle Says

Have you ever thought about why cats have such expressive ears? It's because we don't have eyebrows.

I suggest that you settle
in for a very long
period of sulking.

Dear Repulsed,

Your description of this cat was a little puzzling at first. Then it dawned on me: deformed ears, stomping feet, caged, ugly... this thing isn't a cat at all. It's something called a rabbit. I have heard rumors, mainly from outdoor cats that live far away from the city, that rabbits make a yummy main course. But since you are a delicate, refined Siamese, it is probably a little too big for you to eat, and its unattractive appearance obviously repels you anyhow. While not exactly criminal, rabbits can be unpleasant at times. Take the foot stomping thing, for example. Actually, you probably should be a little flattered by that, because it means the rabbit is scared of you! In any case, if I were you, I don't think I'd concern myself so much with the rabbit (who is stuck in a cage anyway) as with your human, who has taken advantage of your good nature by bringing it into your home. I suggest that you settle in for a very long period of sulking, food shunning, and refusing to allow your human to touch you. Tear up a few pieces of furniture while you are at it to underscore your unhappiness. And since you Siamese are talkative types, make sure to tell off your human every chance you get. You may not be able to convince her to get rid of the rabbit, but she will certainly think twice before bringing home any more of these horrible animals. 🐾

From Grief to Grievance

Dear Sparkle,

For most of my fifteen years, I lived with my best friend, a gray tabby like me. We were adopted from the humane society when we were kittens. But a few weeks ago, my friend got very ill and died. I was grief-stricken and very depressed. Well, a week barely went by before my human decided I needed a "new friend" and brought home a six-month-old kitten, as if any cat from the humane society could replace my closest companion! As you might guess, I am not too fond of this kitten. I can't turn a corner without getting jumped by him. He tore up my two toy mice and my human has gotten him about a half-dozen more cat toys, all of which he is destroying one by one. I'm really not in the mood for a "new friend," and besides, this kitten is really irritating. I'm not young anymore, but I'm really tempted to run away. What do you think?

Signed,

MiSERaBLE

You are stuck with the results
of your human's unthinking.

Dear Miserable,

Don't run away, unless you just escape and hide under the house overnight. That'll put some fear into your human and teach her a lesson for trying to replace one cat with another—and lying to you. The truth is that she wasn't getting *you* a "new friend;" she was getting herself another cat! Humans don't mean to lie. In fact, your human might be lying to herself about her motives in dashing off to the humane society mere days after the death of your best friend. If she were honest with herself, she'd admit that she got a new kitten to inject some youth and life into a house that probably seemed rather bleak and depressing. Now you are stuck with the results of your human's unthinking and impetuous whim. Here's what I suggest: hide a lot. Show up late for dinner, if at all. Your human will wonder if something's wrong with you. Hopefully, she'll call the vet before actually taking you down there, and the vet will probably explain that you are depressed over your friend's death, and this new kitten has turned your life upside down even further. If this tactic doesn't make your human pay more attention to you and give you some space to escape the annoying kitten, then disappearing under the house overnight might be the next best move. As for the kitten, give him some time. You may never be best buddies, but at least his irritating antics will lessen as he matures. 🐾

Python Pique

Dear Sparkle,

My human just got the most boring pet
ever. It's all one long body with no legs
and it doesn't move around very much. He
calls this thing a snake and he spends
way too much time doting on it. It took
him forever to set up the glass room
the snake lives in, decorating it, making sure it's warm enough, etc. But I'm
really galled by what he gives this snake
to eat—dead rats! He takes them out of
the freezer, thaws them out and gives
them to this dumb creature. And what do
you think I get? Yep, plain old canned
cat food. How come I don't get the cool,
dead rats? I think I'm being gypped here.

Signed,

Wishing for Rodents

Dear Wishing,

Like you, I don't get why any human would want to keep snakes as pets. All they ever do is sleep and slither around a bit. They don't do cool things like chase toys or purr or attack humans' feet under the bed sheets. So I can't blame you for being jealous that this snake gets better meals than you do. Actually, I have heard of some people feeding their cats the frozen feeder mice and rats meant for snakes, but raw food people and vets are still debating about whether that's a good idea. Personally, I think coveting a snake's dead mice is pointless when you can do something this caged-up creature can't: you can hunt your own live prey. Which would you rather have: a recently defrosted rodent or a still warm, freshly killed one? And if there aren't a lot of rats or mice in your neighborhood—say, if you're confined to an apartment—you can still hunt down beetles, moths, and crickets. A lizard snuck into our house once (unfortunately I was so stunned by my good fortune, my human caught him before I could). The only thing I *don't* suggest you stalk is the snake. Your human, deluded as he may be, is clearly attached to it. And if it is quite large, it might consider *you* prey—bet you didn't think of that, did you? So stay clear of the serpent. 🐾

Not Pleased to Meet You

Dear Sparkle,

After living at a cat rescue for six months, I have a new home, but I'm not sure I'm happy here. The humans are very nice and treat me very well—good food, treats, fun toys. But there's another cat here and he hates me! What's worse, even though we are both full-grown, he's twice my size. Every time he sees me, he growls and yowls and chases me. If he manages to catch me, he bites me on the back of the neck until I scream, or until one of the humans sprays him with a water bottle (which usually gets me wet in the process too). This cat is making my life miserable. Most of the day I have to hide behind the dresser—he's too big to get back there. Sometimes I can get around while he's napping, if I'm quiet and don't get too near him. I hate living like this. Even with all the good stuff here, I am tempted to run away. Is there *anything* I can do?

Signed,

Picked On

I'd suggest you tough it out
instead of running away.

Dear Picked On,

Before you blame your unfortunate situation on the other cat, walk in his paws for a moment. He's been there a while and has his litter box, his scent marks, and his humans arranged how he wants—then you show up. Suddenly nothing smells right and he has to share everything with you, some strange cat. Even worse, every time he shows his frustration, he gets punished. Maybe you wouldn't behave quite as violently, but you would still be extremely unhappy. The problem is that your humans, well meaning as they are, didn't introduce the two of you correctly. It sounds like they brought you home, dumped you in the middle of the living room and expected everything to be fine—and of course it wasn't. Smart humans orchestrate introductions by giving the new cat her own temporary room, separate from the rest of the house, and bribing the cat who's already there with treats and toys to make the new cat's presence palatable. If your humans wise up, they will return to square one and start introductions all over again. If they do nothing, or the bully never accepts you, I'd suggest you tough it out instead of running away. Your humans probably won't let you suffer forever and will either find you a new home, or at the very least return you to the cat rescue so you can get rehomed from there. 🐾

Cat vs. Human

Sometimes I wonder why we cats have chosen to live with these large, furless creatures known as humans. They're clumsy, not very bright, and they expect every other creature to speak Human. It's a rare occurrence when one of them even attempts to learn the most basic Cat language. So no wonder there's such a huge communication breakdown between cats and humans. Usually when there's a difference of opinion, the cat will win because of our tenaciousness. But every so often a human comes along who just refuses to get it. That's when letters, such as those in this chapter, will pop up in my mailbox.

Nauseous Interruptus

Dear Sparkle,

As you know, the puking thing is one of the not-so-fun aspects of being a kitty, but my human makes it even worse for me. The moment I start heaving because I'm about to upchuck my dinner or hack up a hairball, she makes a grab for me! According to her, I'm only supposed to puke in special places. Like, apparently the carpet is off limits and so is the hardwood floor. Do you know what it's like to be grabbed around the middle and pulled around when you're feeling sick to your stomach? If I see her coming I try to run away, which is also rather difficult to accomplish when you're hacking. How can I get my human to leave me alone while I'm trying to perform this natural, but rather unpleasant kitty function?

Signed,

QUEASY

Sparkle Says

Humans just don't get it: cat fur is a badge of honor to be worn proudly.

It's best to throw up
when your human
is not around.

Dear Queasy,

It seems like whenever a cat gets ready to vomit, humans go into an uproar. You'd think the house was caving in, the way they behaved! We're already feeling icky, and here's some human, all upset because all she can think about is cleaning up the "mess." It's just more proof that humans think only of themselves and their own convenience. And trying to train them out of their selfish behavior is practically impossible, at least with this particular issue. Ideally, it's best to throw up when your human is not around—either while she's out of the house, or in another part of the house far, far away from you. I know this isn't always possible—when you've got to puke, you've got to puke—but if you can swing it, at least you will have some peace while you're doing it. My second suggestion is for those times when you can't avoid her and she tries grabbing you. Instead of puking on the floor, puke on *her*—aim for her shoes, her pants, or even better, her blouse, especially if it's one of those blouses she has to take to the place she calls the "dry cleaners." Of course, it will seem like an accident, and she won't hold you accountable. But the important thing is that she will probably let go of you, and you'll have a couple of brief moments to escape and finish throwing up while she's otherwise occupied. 🐾

Couch Conflict

Dear Sparkle,

This human brought me home from the local rescue, so I'm still getting used to things around here. Some of it's nice— great cat food and a cool cat tree that's taller than my new human. But there are other things I'm not so sure about, like the ongoing debate my human and I have been having over the couch. For some unknown reason, she wants me to stay off it, but it's the best perch in the house! It catches the afternoon sun just right, and it's an even more comfortable place to nap than the cat tree is. I hate to tell my human, but I ain't giving it up! So how to I make her stop shooing me away every time I try to settle down for a nice, sunny nap?

Signed,

Couch Potato

The couch is your
territory.

Dear C. Potato,

When it comes to getting something we really want, we cats will always outlast humans. Trust me, that couch is *all yours.* But you already know that. You're going to keep jumping up on it until your human lets you be. It's a process, and there's really no way to shorten the time frame. Just keep on doing what you're doing. Eventually the nagging will stop.

Don't let this inevitability lure you into complacency, however. Your human will pull a few surprises, but there are always "work-arounds." If she thinks you will shed on the couch, she might toss a throw over it. This could be a good thing. Throws are comfy, and they also indicate that you've won the battle, as long as you lie on them, not the bare couch. If your human worries that you will sharpen your claws on the couch, she may use "Sticky Paws," a two-sided tape that feels gross under our paws. Don't step on it! At least not until you've rubbed all over it and covered up the stickiness with your fur. Then the Sticky Paws tape will smell like you and let the world know the couch is yours.

As for direct confrontations with your human (her yelling, that dreaded spray bottle, etc.), just do most of your couch sitting when she isn't home, but let her catch you often enough to make her realize that the couch is your territory. 🐾

Boyfriend Blues

Dear Sparkle,

My human and I live by ourselves in a big apartment that overlooks a yard that attracts lots of birds. I think our life is perfect, but my human apparently doesn't agree because lately she's been seeing this guy—a lot! Sometimes she's gone all night. Other times, he comes over and stays overnight. I don't like this guy. He's big and loud and obnoxious and he smells funny. He watches noisy things on TV, with people screaming a lot. Sometimes *he* screams at the TV. He's very strange and I don't know what my human sees in him. He's not mean to me or anything; in fact, I usually hang out under the bed while he's around so I don't see all that much of him. But my human's talking like she wants to move in with him, which means we would have to leave this cool apartment! This guy has to go. Any tips on what to do?

Signed,

Concerned

Give him a few cautious sniffs
(try not to wrinkle your nose).

Dear Concerned,

I know how worrisome new humans can be, and this one is turning your own human into a nitwit. That said, you might be jumping to conclusions. Male humans hate change nearly as much as we cats do, so he may not be in any hurry to make a new home with you and your human. In fact, if he is slow enough, maybe your human will stop seeing him. In the meantime, check him out. Get out from under the bed and give him a few cautious sniffs (try not to wrinkle your nose). Hopefully he's not one of those obnoxious types who immediately grabs for you. If he does, scoot right back under the bed until he learns some manners. If he acknowledges your presence but lets you be, that's good. Worse case scenario is if he pushes you away. Then do what you can to get rid of him—pee on his clothes or chew on his shoes. But if he behaves himself, take some time to get to know him. Maybe your human will even encourage him to give you treats or play with you. The situation *can* be manipulated in your favor.

As for the moving part, it's possible you could wind up in a bigger home with a yard that has a better selection of birds than what you already have. Who knows? So just keep a watchful eye on the situation. That should give you a better idea on how to proceed. 🐾

Easy Reader

Dear Sparkle,

Whenever I want to lie on top of a magazine or a book, my human insists on reading it. Literally, we're talking every time I try to flop down on some cool, crinkly paper, it happens—I get shoved off it. What is with that? Do all humans do it? How can I get mine to stop reading the magazines and books that I enjoy sitting on?

Signed,

Literary Loafer

Sparkle Says

Kitty Tip #59: Whatever you want, a soft-spoken "meep" will usually get it for you.

Dear Literary Loafer,

This weird human habit is not really all that mysterious, if you give it some thought. Humans only pull out magazines or books when they want to read them. They put them away when they are done. And you can't just go to the bookcase or magazine stack and browse around for things to lie on. It's more convenient to wait for your human to do it for you. So there you have the conflict. The funny thing about this is that humans wonder why *we* lie on magazines and books when *they* are trying to read them! And they come up with some hilarious theories—for example, they think we do it for attention (naturally, it has to be *all about them*). Ha! They should try leaving a few magazines sitting around on the bed or their couch for a few days instead of putting them away. They'll notice that we lie on them even when there are no humans around at all. Unfortunately, there's not much you can do to keep your human from reading the books and magazines that you want to use for your own purposes. Humans are very possessive creatures and they believe that these things belong to them. You will just have to be more persistent with lying on your magazines and books than your human is in reading them. If you keep coming back, she'll give up and go read something else. 🐾

Nickname Nightmare

Dear Sparkle,

When my human brought me home, she decided to call me Max, which I thought was a fairly decent name. I even come when I hear her say it (usually that means she has some food for me). But now that we've been living together for a few months, she has started to call me some wacky versions of my name—Maxie-Boy, Maxie-Baxie, Mad Max, and the worst, Maxie-Boo-Boo-Baby. It's disgusting, not to mention undignified. I am MAX, M-A-X, no "Boo," no "Baby," and I'm only "Mad" Max when she starts messing with my name! How can I keep her from mangling my perfectly decent name?

Signed,

Just Max

When your human
mangles your name,
make yourself scarce.

Dear Max,

Silly kitty! The answer to your problem is obvious. Every time your human starts mangling your name, make yourself scarce. Only show up when she uses your proper name. You do have to be consistent about this. The big mistake cats make is responding to a nickname at dinnertime or when their humans are being nice to them. Doing this only encourages them to keep using it. If you want to be called Max, then only respond to Max. When your human uses one of those other, unsatisfactory names, walk away, no matter how tempting it is to stick around and be petted, and no matter how hungry you are. Yes, you may have to miss out on a few dinners while your human wanders around your home, calling out, "Maxie-Boo-Boo-Baby, where *are* yooouuuu?" but unless you want that as your permanent name, you'd better stay hunkered down in the closet or in the darkest part of the guest room. The penchant for hideous nicknames is almost an addiction with humans, and they even do it to each other. You need to make it 100 percent clear that you don't play that game, or you'll be stuck in a never-ending version of it. 🐾

Carried Away

Dear Sparkle,

Like any self-respecting cat, I hate going
to the vet. Just try shoving me in that
horrible carrier thing and see what happens! I'll be under the bed in a flash. My
escape tactics to avoid these horrible vet
visits worked quite well for a very long
time. Then my human tricked me! She left
the carrier thing out for weeks, and then
she started putting my food nearby. She
even tossed a couple of my favorite catnip
toys inside it. After all this, my guard
was down, and one day, she suddenly shoved
me in the carrier! Next thing I knew I was
at the vet's, getting prodded with a ther-
mometer and stuck with a needle. It was
humiliating! I cannot let this happen again! Any advice?

Signed,

Mortified

Sparkle Says

My idea for vet care
reform: put the vets
into carriers and bring
them to us instead of
vice versa.

Maybe you should use the cat carrier as a litter box.

Dear Mortified,

I could be Miss Goody Four-Paws, say that it's important to have regular vet checkups, and tell you to just suck it up and deal with having to be in the carrier occasionally. But that would be ignoring two things: 1) I'm not that kind of kitty, and 2) your human spent a lot of time and effort to trick you into thinking that carrier was part of your own personal furniture. That was pretty underhanded of her, even though I'm sure she believes she did it with your best interest in mind (i.e., making you less "stressed out" about the carrier). You should show her that "no good deed goes unpunished." (I'm not sure where that quote came from, but whichever human said it, she must have been a bit feline herself.) So your human wanted you to be comfortable with that cat carrier, eh? If she went to that much trouble to make you feel at home in it, maybe you should show her how grateful you are for all her efforts and use it as a litter box. That would really prove that you have accepted this cat carrier as your very own piece of furniture, to do with as you wish. Or you could just take the easy way out and refuse to go within ten feet of it, no matter what temptations your human gives you. I call this the "lazy cat's option," but then, that includes the majority of us, doesn't it? 🐾

Affection Rejection

Dear Sparkle,

My human is really pretty cool. She is my best friend and she gives me lots of toys and treats. I want to show her how much I appreciate her, so I love giving her little licks and kisses. But here's the problem—she rejects my displays of affection! Whenever I lick her, she pushes me away and tries to make me stop. She says my tongue is too rough and my breath smells (like hers doesn't, especially first thing in the morning). You can imagine how much this hurts my feelings. At first I thought maybe I caught her at the wrong time and she was just in a bad mood, but she complains every time I try to get affectionate with her. Are all humans like this, or do you think there is a problem between us that she isn't telling me?

Signed,

A Lover and a Licker

You picked a picky human.

Dear Licker,

When it comes to licking, some humans like it and some don't, just as some cats do it and some don't. My human, for example, would give anything to have me lick her and I won't do it. I'm just not into licking humans, only other cats. My roommate Binga, on the other hand, loves to lick humans. She even licks the dog (yeech!). And nobody here ever complains about her. You just picked a picky human. Some of them are like that. Their skin is sensitive to the smallest irritation and the tiniest unpleasant smell sends them searching for an air freshener. I bet she also puts deodorizer in your litter box, wrinkles her nose whenever she gives you canned food, and washes her hands or face the second you try to lick them.

I'm afraid there's not much you can do to change your human. Some things you can train them to do—feed you at certain times, change your litter box frequently, and give you cat trees, for example—but other qualities are just hardwired into their personalities. Hypersensitivity is one of them. You'll just have to appreciate all the other, good things she does for you without being so physical about it. I purr and give headbutts myself; maybe you should try that. But I do have to say that if I were stuck with a finicky human like yours I would be inclined to give her a swift bite on the nose instead. 🐾

Entitlement Trouble

Dear Sparkle,

I really need your advice because my humans are abusing me! They give me whatever canned food they decide is okay, even if it's not my favorite. I've had the same kitty condo for three years now—not that I want this one to be replaced. I want a second one to go with the first, but they won't get it for me. I tried to scratch the couch in protest but they covered it with that gross double-sided sticky tape stuff. Plus, I only get treats once a day, and sometimes my litter box goes for a whole day before it gets changed. And it gets worse—my humans brush me several times a week, which I hate, and if I'm lying on the couch and they want to watch the television, they pick me up and put me in my own bed! So I need to know how to get in contact with the ASPCA. Do you think they can find me a better set of humans?

Signed,

Outraged

The less you act like
   you care, the more
   your humans will care.

Dear Outraged,

I am all for getting the tastiest food, unlimited treats, and having multiple kitty condos, but the lack of any of the above is not abuse, at least not to the ASPCA. They're more concerned with homeless kitties, or abuse that involves physical injury. The ASPCA would only laugh at your complaints. You *are* entitled to the things you want, but you're going about it the wrong way. Let me explain.

Cats expect things to be exactly as we want them, and there's a certain magic in that. Because we already assume our favorite food is in the cupboard, or that second cat condo is out there just waiting to be claimed, our humans conclude that they must give them to us. When a cat demands what he wants, as you are doing, the assumption is that you *don't* have it yet—otherwise, why would you need to demand it? That's when your humans realize that they can say no. Even worse, when they get it for you, they may expect you to be grateful! Gratitude should never be in a cat's vocabulary. When you expect something to be there, no gratitude is necessary.

If you detach yourself from your humans and their frivolous whims, they will twist themselves inside out to please you. It sounds backwards, but the less you act like you care, the more your humans *will* care. Try it out for a few weeks—you'll see that I'm right. 🐾

Impractical Jokester

Dear Sparkle,

My human has no sense of humor! She gets
upset at the stupidest little things.
For example, the two of us live by ourselves, and whenever she goes into the
bathroom she leaves the door open. So
unlike a lot of you other cats, I'm not
faced with a shut door. Cool, right? So
I always take advantage of the situation and walk right in after her. Usually she doesn't mind, except when she's
using the human litter box. I have this
game, see—whenever she's sitting there,
I sneak around the back and whap at
her from behind! This always makes her
scream, which is really fun, but then
she gets mad at me like I've done something wrong. What's the matter with her?
Why can't she just laugh it off along
with me?

Signed,

Playful but Perturbed

A cat's most charming trait should be unpredictability.

Dear Playful,

This proves that even the most fortunate situation has a downside. Although you never have to face a shut bathroom door, your human takes your little practical joke with less than good humor. Maybe your behavior *isn't* all that funny. How would *you* feel if your human crept up behind you in your own litter box and pulled your tail? You wouldn't like that, would you? You might even stop using your litter box altogether. It's a good thing you haven't put your human off *her* litter box—imagine how awful that would be!

I should also remind you: for all their size, humans can be surprisingly fragile, mainly because of their lack of a fur covering. When you slap at your human from behind, you could be causing her pain. Claws hurt bare skin, although they would barely make a dent in another cat. So your little joke is an unpleasant surprise to your human on several different levels.

If you're going to keep whacking at your human, consider keeping your claws retracted. Make it more of a poke than an all-out *whap!* Even with this modification she may start doing the unthinkable and shutting the door when she's using the porcelain litter box. Indulge in it only sporadically. Let her forget about it for a while, just to make sure the bathroom door remains open. One of a cat's most charming traits should always be her unpredictability. 🐾

Offensive Oratory

Dear Sparkle,

My human is addicted to that phone thing and she is always talking on it. That wouldn't be so bad—I'm part Siamese, so I enjoy a good conversation too—except that she has the most annoying voice ever! She'll be yammering on for hours and laughing that shrill, ear-piercing laugh. It's unbearable! So I start poking her and screaming at her to shut up, but it never works. In fact, she's flattered because she thinks I want to get in on her chats. Trust me, I don't. She talks about boring things like diets and men and clothes—things that don't interest cats in the least. What I want is for her to talk more quietly, and in a lower tone of voice. Is there anything I can do to make myself clear?

Signed,

Sore Ears

She'll learn that when
you start howling it's
time for her to shut up.

Dear Sore Ears,

Since your human is clueless about how awful her voice is and you can't tell her she should work on making it more pleasant, your only alternative is to figure out how to make her shut up. You can't do the usual tricks to make her stop what she's doing, such as knocking something over or shredding the sofa, because she will yell in an even louder voice. My suggestion is to "fight fire with fire," as the human cliché goes. When your human's annoying chattering has gone on for too long, crawl under the bed and start howling. Really make it sound like you are in pain (which you probably are from her obnoxious laughter). She'll think something's wrong and get off the phone so she can check up on you. Continue crouching under the bed, howling, until she has spent a good ten minutes trying to comfort you—that will guarantee that she hasn't merely left the other party on hold. When you have her full attention, come out from under the bed, purring loudly, and rub up against her. See, you are rewarding her for getting off the phone. If you do this repeatedly, she will eventually learn that when you start howling it is time for her to remove the phone from her ear and shut up. Yes, this is a lot of effort, but it is worth it if her voice if half as grating as you have implied. 🐾

Un-Easy Chair

Dear Sparkle,

My favorite piece of furniture in the whole house is a big chair that's covered with the most delightful, nubby fabric. It's also my human's favorite piece of furniture. But we like it for different reasons, and it's causing a conflict between us. She likes to sit in it and play with the square plastic thing she calls a laptop or watch the bigger screen with the fun moving images on it. I like it because the nubby fabric is the perfect scratching surface! Seriously I could dig my claws into it all day, if my human didn't yell at me every time I tried to do it. I don't understand why she gets upset since I don't scratch any of the areas she sits on. It seems like we should be able to share our favorite chair. How can I make her see the light?

Signed,

Scratching My Head—and Chair

Sparkle Says

Why is it that humans go around destroying the planet, and then yell at us cats for clawing their furniture?

Humans are so weird
about chairs . . . they
hate sharing them.

Dear Scratching,

Humans are so weird about chairs and sofas. They hate sharing them. I don't get it either. As you pointed out, you can get your enjoyment by clawing the parts of it that your human never uses—and she gets mad anyway. It must be some sort of strange possessive instinct. If that's it, I can't say I blame them too much. In a multi-cat family, a certain amount of negotiation always goes on when a new cat tree arrives, and the tree generally belongs to one cat more than it does to the others. Speaking of cat trees, I'm assuming you don't have one, otherwise you would probably be scratching it instead of the chair. Either that, or the cat tree's scratching surfaces are nowhere near as satisfying as the material on the chair. That nubby stuff does rule—they should cover a cat tree in that instead of carpet. If your human really wanted to keep you from clawing her beloved chair, she should have gotten one covered in microfiber and given you your own cat tree, covered in your choice of scratching fabric. Unfortunately, only a shockingly small percentage of humans have that type of foresight. So your best bet is to use the chair when your human isn't in it, and preferably when she isn't home at all, so you won't be disturbed. 🐾

Night Shift

Dear Sparkle,

When my humans go to sleep, they shut the
bedroom door. I find this unsatisfactory.
Eleven o'clock at night is prime playtime! Why would anyone go to bed at that
hour? So I do what any normal cat would
do—I meow loudly and scratch at the door.
They ignored me for a few days so I caused
more of a racket, figuring that they would
come out and toss some toys around. But do
you know what they did instead? They gave
me food! I didn't really want the food
but I ate some of it anyway. I mean it
was there, right? After a few bites I got
bored, so I scratched and meowed again.
Then the humans did something terrible—
they took me to the vet! Apparently they
thought that I was sick, but of course
I checked out fine. Then the vet also told
them I weighed enough as it was and not to
leave me any food at night. Clearly, these
people are clueless. I want playtime! Is
there any way to get my point across?

Signed,

Going Nuts

You actually have to show
them what you want.

Dear Nuts,

Because humans function at such a low level of comprehension, you need to really be obvious with them. I mean, it's clear to you and me what you want by carrying on the way you do at eleven P.M., but they'll never get it. Not in a million years (human *or* cat years). So instead of just scratching and meowing, you have to actually *show* them what you want. Do you have a lot of toys sitting around the house? Gather them up and set them by the bedroom door before you start making noise. That way, when they open the door, the toys will be right there in their faces. Once I actually got my human's attention by taking a toy and flinging it against the shut door several times. You may want to try the same thing, or at least toss one or two of the toys in the air the moment the humans open the door. I know it sounds like a lot of effort when you're asking for something so simple, but what can I say? Even the most well intentioned humans, like yours, are hopelessly dense. If your humans were really smart, they would play with you for a little while *before* going to bed. Then maybe you wouldn't need to bother them after they've turned in. Too bad you can't tell them that. 🐾

One Cat World

Dear Sparkle,

I live with my human and no other cats and I like it that way. Once she tried to bring home another cat and I wasn't having any! I refused to let that cat anywhere near the food or the litter box and she had to be confined to her own room so I couldn't beat her up. Finally my human took her away, much to my relief. So things have been fine until recently. There have been no other cats, but at least once a week, sometimes more often, I smell them on my human's clothes and hands. The weird thing is that it always seems to be a different cat that I smell! Often it's the scent of several cats intermingled. As you can imagine, I'm very unhappy with this. The moment that strange cat smell reaches my nostrils I growl, dash under the bed, and refuse to talk to my human for a couple of hours. What is up with her? Where is she finding these other cats and why is she hanging out with them?

Signed,

KITTY-IN-CHIEF

You are an only kitty
and your human wants
a clowder of cats.

Dear K-I-C,

A little on the dominant side, aren't we? Demanding to be the only cat your human is ever around may be asking a little much of her. Here's why.

Most cats assume that there are two kinds of humans: cat humans and non-cat humans. But in reality, there are different levels of cat humans. Some are most comfortable bonding with just one special kitty. Then there are multi-cat humans, who need two, three, or more cats to make up a happy family. Your human probably falls into the latter category. So you and your human are a little mismatched: you are vehemently an only kitty and she wants a clowder of cats. Since your human is frustrated living in an only-cat home, she might be volunteering at a cat rescue or shelter. That would explain why she rarely smells like the same cat and sometimes smells like several. Rescues always have cats coming and going, so she probably hangs out with different cats there. That's my best guess.

While I know you would like your human to cease whatever activity is bringing her in contact with all those other cats, maybe it's for the best. She gets her multi-cat fix and then she comes home to just you. If she would stop rubbing it in by smelling to high heaven and maybe bring home some catnip in the bargain, however, it *would* make a nice peace offering. 🐾

Epi-Curious

You would think that since we have our own personal chefs and meal servers that food would not be an issue for us cats. But no! Humans mess with our mealtimes in ways that are downright creative! They are particularly hard to train in this area, and if a cat isn't diligent, she will wind up with late dinners, slopped together dishes of unappealing fare, and—heaven forbid!—no in-between meal treats. Yes, meal management can be one of the most challenging aspects of a cat's canon, but it's also one of the most rewarding, so I am always happy to help out when a fellow feline finds herself in a fix.

Meal Mix-Up

Dear Sparkle,

Like most cats, my roommate and I consider dinnertime to be one of the highlights of the day. But my human seems intent on ruining things for us. She puts down our food and it always goes the same way. I eat some of mine and my roommate eats some of hers, then we check out each other's food bowls. Usually it's the same stuff in both our dishes, so it really doesn't matter which one we eat out of. But my human disagrees with us and gets mad when we switch bowls. What's her problem? It's not like we're eating any of *her* food!

Signed,

No Dining Dibs Here

It is your right as a cat
to examine any food
you are able to reach.

Dear NDDH,

It sounds like you have one of those humans who likes everything "just so." She's probably one of those neatness freaks who has a place for everything and who lives by some idiotic "schedule." The good part of that is your meals will never be late. The bad part is that she thinks dinner has to go a certain way or it's not being done right. Ha! And *we're* called creatures of habit! Honestly, if it's the same kind of food in each dish and you both eat about the same amount, I don't see what she's complaining about. On the other hand, if one of you needs more food than the other, or if you or your roommate has to eat a special diet, then she's still the one who's in the wrong for feeding you together. Does she expect you to police yourselves? Hello! That's not your job as kitties. Your job is to look cute and eat what is put in front of you—and check out anyone else's dinner that is nearby. In fact, it is your absolute right as a cat to examine *any* food you are able to reach. If you and your roommate are on different diets, your human should separate you at dinnertime. If it's the same food in both dishes, she should suck it up and stop whining. And you can tell her I said so. 🐾

No Compliments to the Chef

Dear Sparkle,

I hate the food my humans give me. Hate it with a passion! It tastes metallic and stale and I can barely wolf it down. In fact, most days, after a few bites, I'll just pretend to bury it and walk away. For some reason, my humans don't get how badly this food blows. At least I assume they don't, since they keep on giving it to me. I'm forced to supplement my meals with tidbits I've begged from the humans at their dinnertime or by jumping on the kitchen counter and eating off their plates before they do the dishes (*please* don't tell them I do this!). You'd think that by trying to bury this awful food, I could get the word out to my humans that things have to change. But they're oblivious. Is there something else I could do to make it more obvious?

Signed,

Foodie Feline

Sparkle Says

Why is there no mouse-flavored cat food? The cat food companies claim the test cats rejected it. Real reason: humans don't know how to properly prepare mouse. Hint—it is best served raw, with organ meat on top.

Refuse to show up at
dinnertime at all.

Dear Foodie,

I agree. It's neglectful of your humans to force this hateful food on you. In fact, it borders on cruelty! How would *they* feel if they were given a diet of, say, liver, lima beans, and Brussels sprouts for the rest of their lives? It would zap the joy right out of their existence. So things must change, but just *how* to change them is another dilemma altogether. First off, you should figure out a better way to bring this matter to their attention. Pretending to bury the food isn't doing it, so you will have to try something else that they can't ignore. How about spreading the food all over the kitchen floor so they step in it? Or how about picking up some morsels—carefully, so you don't accidentally swallow them—and dropping them on your humans' food while they're eating dinner? The latter trick might not be all that helpful (they may even think you are trying to share your dinner with them), but it will ruin their meal, which will at least give you a crumb of satisfaction. Or you could refuse to show up for dinnertime at all and avoid your food altogether. If you won't even look at it, much less touch or taste it, your humans will finally realize they are "wasting their money" (something humans hate with a passion), and they'll be more inclined to get you a different brand. 🐾

Bug Banquet

Dear Sparkle,

The meals around here are pretty good, but sometimes I feel like supplementing my diet with something freshly killed, so I'll snag a fly or a beetle, or sometimes one of those fluffy moths you always rave about (and I have to admit, they are pretty tasty!). These bugs are full of nutrients and protein. They make an excellent supplement to what I already eat, and I think my human would enjoy them too. The only problem is that she doesn't seem to understand that. I've caught bugs for her several times and all she does is scream when I show up with them—talk about unappreciative! Once I tried making a surprise of it and left a big, succulent grasshopper on her pillow. She didn't like that at all! Okay, so I admit I kind of chewed on it and ate one of the legs first—was that so wrong? If I try again, do you think she will like it better if I leave it whole?

Signed,

Insect Aficionado

Don't waste bugs on your human. Save them for yourself.

Dear Insect Aficionado,

It's a rare cat that gives thought to the nutrition of the food he consumes. It's even rarer for a cat to care about the nutrition of his human's diet (although I have met a few). But there is something that's even rarer than that. In fact, I don't even know if such a thing exists: a human who will eat the bugs that her cat catches for her. I hate to tell you this, but no matter how nicely you present it, or how sincere your intent is, your human will never accept your gifts with anything but revulsion. Yes, it's very, very rude of her, but you can't help her manners, either. Humans eat a lot of things that seem strange to us cats— tomatoes, strawberry shortcake, and granola, to name a few of their more curious choices. Fortunately, humans don't try to force these things on us, and in return they don't want us offering them our favorite delicacies either. Honestly, I think it is rather close-minded of humans. At least we cats will sniff something before rejecting it. Humans will cringe and scream before they have even had a chance to smell a dead insect, so they don't even know it if might appeal to them. Bottom line: I'm sorry, there's nothing you can do about your human's bad taste or lack of social graces. Don't waste any more bugs on her. Save them for yourself. 🐾

Wake Up Call

Dear Sparkle,

We have a scheduling problem at my house. I prefer breakfast to be served at six A.M., but my human doesn't wake up until seven, and then she takes her time shuffling around the kitchen before dishing up my food. Can you give me some suggestions on how to get her up to speed?

Signed,

Early to Rise

Sparkle Says

Things *Not* to Do When Your Cat Is Eating:

- Microwave popcorn
- Construction work
- Argue
- Eat your own meal (wait, so you can share with us)

"You lazy slug,
get me breakfast!"

Dear Early,

The secret to getting your human out of bed is to figure out which stimuli works best. Some react well to an interactive approach—jumping on the bed and generally making things uncomfortable for them. Then there are passive-aggressive tactics, such as licking their faces or touching them with your paw—actions they interpret as affection instead of, "You lazy slug, get me my breakfast!" Then there are more assertive methods—running across the bed, pulling off the covers, and such. Many humans will bolt out of bed when they hear you screaming. Once they are up, there's a better than fifty-fifty chance that they'll stay up; if they go back to bed, just start sounding off again. If none of these tactics work, then you need more extreme measures, such as knocking things off of shelves in as noisy a manner as possible. If your human has become wise to such tricks and shuts you out of the bedroom completely, you'll have to resort to throwing yourself against the door and yowling. Undignified? Yes, but never let a closed door come between you and breakfast. Once your human is up and in the kitchen, stop her lollygagging by getting in the way. Be persistent and soon she will get in the habit of feeding you first thing so you will stop "bothering" her. Any self-respecting cat (and clearly you are one) can accomplish this with one paw tied behind her back. 🐾

Milk Malady

Dear Sparkle,

I think my human is trying to poison me!
She keeps giving me this white liquid that
tastes delicious, but every time I lap it
up, it makes me ill! I get nauseous and
my stomach feels like it's knotted up.
You would think that after the first time
I had this stuff I wouldn't drink it anymore, but I can't help myself. It's just
too good, and my human keeps giving it
to me. Why is she torturing me like this?
It's really cruel.

Signed,

QUEASY QUENTIN

Dear Queasy,

Many cats (and even more humans) have a tendency to enjoy food that isn't good for them. Or at least they enjoy it until it hits their digestive system. From what you've described, I've gathered that it's milk you keep drinking; obviously your human has never gotten the news that many cats are lactose intolerant and that giving them milk will cause an upset stomach. On top of that, she is also so clueless that she doesn't notice that you are unwell after you drink the stuff. If your human were smarter, she would know that most pet stores carry a lactose-free version of milk for cats like you, but at this point I think you should shun anything liquid she gives you unless it is plain water. If you find it impossible to resist the milk you are offered, even though you know how it's going to make you feel, your only alternative is to make her stop giving it to you completely. There is a handy way to do this, and I'm surprised you haven't done this yet. Many times, drinking milk will give a lactose-intolerant cat the runs. So next time this happens, *don't* run for your litter box. Catch my drift? After your human has had to clean up the mess once or twice, I can guarantee that she will not want to give you any more milk. 🐾

Nip Lifter

Dear Sparkle,

Just wait 'til you hear this one! A couple of days ago, without any warning, the humans brought home a puppy. As you might imagine, I was quite annoyed about this. Unlike you and the dog at your house, however, I was starting to consider accepting her. She seems all right, if a bit clumsy and dense. And the humans are being extra nice to me right now (I have trained them well). But disaster has struck! This morning the puppy was wandering around and getting into things, as puppies will do, and she found my catnip stash. And do you know what she did? *She ate it!* The extra-special, extremely potent, high-quality stuff that my humans get from a secret source is *all gone!* When I found out, I was beside myself. Even worse, the humans thought it was funny! They have a very sick sense of humor. I will tolerate just about anything, but my stash is sacred! What can I do?

Signed,

EXASPERATED

Sparkle Says

The fact that dogs are so trainable does *not* make them smarter than us cats. Since when has being easily manipulated become a sign of intelligence?

Teach the puppy
that she can't
mess with you.

Dear Exasperated,

Honestly, aren't you over-reacting just a little? I'm sure your humans will get you more nip. It seems like they are trying hard to stay in your good graces now that there is a dog in the house, even if they did slip by finding your predicament amusing.

But the missing nip isn't your real problem. You need to keep the puppy away from your stuff in general. Puppies are destructive creatures. They get into everything (including, possibly, your litter box) and tear things apart (including, most likely, your cat toys). Your humans, meanwhile, are training the new puppy, but from a human perspective. They are more focused on protecting their things than they are yours. So you have to train the puppy from your own cat perspective. I hope you are up on your boxing moves because you are going to need them. Fluffing up and hissing may give the puppy pause whenever she's near your stuff, but it probably won't completely stop her at first. Fluffing up, hissing, and adding a good one-two wallop most likely will. Repeatedly administering this treatment will help teach the puppy that she can't mess with you and your possessions. Eventually all you will have to do is fluff up and stare her down and she should back off. Puppies need to learn boundaries, and you must be consistent. If you trained your humans, you should find training the puppy a simple process. 🐾

Table Manners

Dear Sparkle,

I'm a cat who likes a bit of variety in her diet. Unfortunately, my humans give me the exact same food, day in and day out. Admittedly, it is good quality and quite tasty, but it gets boring after a while. The humans, on the other hand, eat something different nearly every night—chicken, salmon, lean cuts of beef, all sorts of good stuff. But they never give me any. I thought that maybe they weren't aware of how selfish they are being, so one night I decided to just help myself. I jumped on the table, snatched a succulent piece of ahi tuna, and ran with it! The humans yelled at me, but at least they let me eat the tuna. ("It's ruined anyway," my female human said.) I think their reaction was a bit out of line. Was I all that rude for taking a little bit of tuna, or are they ruder for not ever offering me any?

Signed,

DINNER ENVY

Sparkle Says

Don't be a cheap date: save heavy petting for *after* dinner.

Many cats get
what amounts to
a second dinner.

Dear Dinner Envy,

Of course I am going to side with you—after all, how often do I side with humans? That said, your behavior was a bit gauche, and you could have handled this issue a little more elegantly. Just because your humans show a gross lack of consideration by always feeding you the same food while they enjoy a variety of dishes, it doesn't mean you must stoop to their level. Since you didn't mention it, I am assuming that you never tried asking politely to have some of your humans' dinner. That works often, and many cats have finessed their techniques so expertly that they wind up getting what amounts to a second dinner. Here are the more successful ploys: sitting on your hind legs and poking the human with one paw; purring, putting your front paws on the edge of a chair, and rubbing your head on the human's leg; and staring up plaintively toward the nearest human and letting out the infamous "voiceless meow" (that will get you nearly anything, as long as you are clear about what you want). What doesn't work: walking on the dining room table (humans are jealous they can't do that themselves, so they get mad when you do); jumping on the humans' laps while they're eating; and whining and hitting your human with claws out. Give some of the proven techniques a try. If they don't work, then go ahead and dive bomb the dinner table. Your humans deserve it. 🐾

A Wing and a Preyer

Dear Sparkle,

My dream has always been to catch a bird. Being an indoor-only cat, this goal has always seemed out of my reach. All I could do was watch longingly out the window as birds flew past, perched on the trees nearby and—most frustrating of all—pecked around on the ground below the windowsill. A couple of times, they perched on the windowsill and stared right at me! You can imagine how crazy I went when that happened. But now I think I've finally got the chance to get my claws into a bird, and it's a doozy! My humans brought it home. This bird is almost as big as I am, with a huge beak and lots of red, yellow, and blue plumage. I am so excited! Got any good bird catching tips? And which part do you suggest I eat first once I've caught it—legs or breast?

Signed,

Batty for Birds

This is no mere canary.

Dear Batty,

Hold it right there! You need to stop and think twice before going after that bird. Seriously. Take a good look at it, especially that powerful beak. Check out its claws—they are longer than yours. This is no mere canary. If I am not mistaken, your humans have brought home a type of bird called a macaw. Macaws are a particularly temperamental kind of parrot. Macaws don't take lightly to cats who are looking for an easy meal, and you are likely to run afoul (no pun intended) of that beak. A macaw will nip you—hard!—if you annoy it, and macaws annoy rather easily. Frankly, with a macaw in the house, I'd recommend that you watch your back.

In any case, going after a bird that obviously belongs to your humans is probably not a good idea anyhow. I imagine they would be less than thrilled if you did manage to take it down and have it for dinner. It probably cost them a lot of money (money that would have been far better spent on a new cat tree, frankly), and I don't think they intended it to be an expensive gourmet meal for you. They may even be emotionally attached to the thing, believe it or not! So I'm afraid your treasured dream will have to continue to go unrealized. But don't blame me—blame your humans. They're the birdbrains who brought home the macaw to begin with. 🐾

Doggie Bag

Dear Sparkle,

I live with a dog, but that's not such a bad thing because I love her food. In fact, I think her food tastes way better than the dreck that's supposed to be for me. So after a few bites of my own dinner, I usually ditch it and head over to the dog's dish. For some reason, my human has deemed this unacceptable. I don't understand why. The dog doesn't care. She lets me eat as much of her food as I want. In fact, she likes *my* food better than I do, so I let her have as much of mine as she wants, too. Seems like a good tradeoff to me. What's so wrong with that?

Signed,

FREAKY FOR DOG FOOD

I love dog food too.

Dear Freaky,

I love dog food too, so I can see why you don't understand the harm in trading off, especially since the dog is agreeable. But unfortunately you two *do* need to stick to your own food bowls because you have different nutritional needs. If you look at the way we behave and dogs behave, it's obvious. When a homeless dog is hungry, it digs through a garbage can and consumes everything it can find. A cat, however, will either hunt for birds or mice, but failing that and forced to go through the garbage, she will pick out leftover fish or chicken for her meal. Dogs are *non-obligate* carnivores, which means that while they need a lot of meat in their diet, they also require a good portion of carbohydrates to balance it out, hence their penchant for wolfing down anything that seems remotely food-like to them. We cats, on the other hand are *obligate* carnivores, which means we are obligated to get most of our nutrition from animal protein—small animals, the salmon your human grilled for dinner, etc. If you eat a lot of dog food, you could wind up with nutritional deficiencies and serious health problems. And your food is too rich in protein and calories for the dog. But don't complain to me—complain to the pet food companies. They need to go back to the drawing board and make cat food that dogs don't like and dog food that we cats don't like.

Dinner for One

Dear Sparkle,

Like many cats, I consider my mealtimes sacred. I want them on time, in the same place every day. And I want the same food every time—no experimenting with new stuff just because it has a cute name like "country fish dinner" or "braised lamb stew" (those names are meant to appeal to humans, not cats). I have my human trained on most of this, except for one thing: once she puts the food down, she won't leave me alone! She hangs out trying to pet me while I eat, making it impossible for me to concentrate on my food. It's distracting and I'd really rather be left alone to enjoy my dinner in peace. Is there some way I can make her stop without hurting her feelings too much?

Signed,

Nice but Annoyed

Sparkle Says

Tell your human to ditch that root beer float and make a tuna float instead. To eight ounces chilled tuna juice, add one scoop ground chicken. Top with a dollop of unsweetened whipped cream. Yum!

I'm afraid there's no way
to get around being mean.

Dear Nice but Annoyed,

You *are* the proverbial "nice kitty" for wanting your space while being considerate of your human. Most cats would just stalk off without a second thought, and refuse to return to their food dish until their human had made herself scarce. In fact, you know what? I'm a little stumped at how to solve your problem because I so rarely have to take into consideration what humans feel about anything! Are you *sure* it's important that you don't hurt her feelings? All the sure-fire methods—walking away, light growling, a little "go away" swat with your claws sheathed—are bound to make her feel bad. Humans always take things so personally, as if a cat's every move reflects on their own self-esteem. It's nearly impossible to cater to a human's feelings and still maintain your cat-ness. Especially in this instance—your human is probably petting you (and annoyingly so) while you eat because she read somewhere that it "creates a bond" between you two. Maybe it does with some cats, but you're not one of them. I'm afraid there's no way to get around being mean to her, just momentarily, to make her stop this. The good news is that humans are resilient creatures, and she'll get over her hurt fairly quickly. In time she will understand that your need to be left alone at dinner is just a quirk of yours, and it shouldn't have a lasting impact on your relationship. 🐾

Litter Box Letters

Considering how much humans complain about our litter boxes (especially when we don't use them), you might guess that this would be the longest chapter in the book. But it's not us cats who have litter box issues—we either like ours or we don't, and if we don't, we take our business elsewhere. It's the humans who think that this is a Big Deal. When I get letters from cats about their litter boxes, it is usually because their humans are having some weird issues about the confounded things. Just wait 'til you hear some of the weird behavior they exhibit over something that should be a cat's private matter!

Technophobe

Dear Sparkle,

My human just got one of those "automatic" litter boxes and I'm not sure I like it. It's oversized, but the actual part with the litter is smaller than my old box. And the thing is spooky—I'll use it and then a little while later, the contraption starts moving! It's kind of scary. I do have to say that I like the fact that it gets rid of the waste far more quickly than my human did. Sometimes she wouldn't scoop my litter box all day, and it was really disgusting. Since she doesn't have to scoop anymore, she's acting like this thing is best idea ever. To be honest, I'm a little peeved that she's so pleased with it. It's not like she's the one who has to actually use it. Do you think I should just accept this new litter box, even though it doesn't really benefit me, or should I show my human how annoyed I am with her for disrupting my routine?

Signed,

Creeped Out

I would carefully weigh both the good and the bad of the automatic litter box.

Dear Creeped Out,

I know all about those automatic litter boxes—we have one here too. I don't use it if I can help it—my human has provided me with an old fashioned box that is much nicer, and in a better location, too. Why should I use something just because it's a convenience for my human? That said, the fact that the automatic litter box is self-cleaning *does* benefit you, not just your human. One thing you have to understand about humans— you can't change them. Of course, in a perfect world, your human would be standing there, waiting to scoop out the litter box every time you used it. But let's face it, that's not gonna happen. This automatic litter box, however, will scoop a few minutes after you've been there. So just because your human worships this new thing, don't immediately write it off. If I were you, I would carefully weigh both the good and the bad of the automatic litter box. That way, you can make a wise decision on whether to accept it or not. Trust me, if you decide you don't like it after all and let your human know that in no uncertain terms, she will be very, very quick to replace it with something more acceptable. 🐾

The Not-so-Great Outdoors

Dear Sparkle,

My sleazebag owner abandoned me when he
moved away, and his neighbors rescued me.
I've convinced them to let me come and go
as I please, but just because I hang around
outside a lot, they expect me to go to the
bathroom there. The thing is I don't want
to! They started off having a litter box
for me, but once they began letting me out,
they took it away. It was very confusing
when I came in and found it gone, so I did
the most logical thing (well, logical considering how badly I needed to go). I went
on the spot where the litter box used to
be. For some reason, the humans were really
bothered by this, but frankly, I think
I should have been the one complaining. Is there something I can do
to make these humans bring back
my litter box?

Signed,

Confounded

Sparkle Says

The Unblinking Kitty
Stare: a good way to
unnerve your humans
and keep them on
their toes.

Look at your humans accusingly. Complain loudly. Circle the area and paw at it.

Dear Confounded,

Your humans took your litter box, assuming you would merely go outside to take care of business. Instead they've inconvenienced you and caused you grief. How would *they* like it if one morning they woke up to discover someone had taken away *their* bathroom? You can bet you would never hear the end of it! While these humans are good-hearted, they aren't very bright, so you may need to work extra hard to, shall we say, *inspire* them to do what's right. You might try virtually taking up residence at the old spot where your litter box used to be. Every time you return from your rounds outdoors, make a beeline for that spot and just sit there, looking at your humans accusingly. Complain loudly. Circle around the area, sniff and paw at it a few times. You don't have to actually *do* anything—in fact, it's even better if you don't, because just the thought that you *might* will stress them out even more than if you actually did. I call it "Siamese water torture." Your unrelenting attention to the former home of your litter box will eventually reduce your humans to quivering masses of servitude. They will do anything to make you stop behaving so oddly. And that includes returning your litter box to its rightful place. At least that's what this tactic should do. If your humans still can't figure it out, then perhaps a few strategically placed "presents" will be in order. 🐾

Litterless Lavatory

Dear Sparkle,

We are two very well-behaved kitties and we cannot understand why our human gets mad at us. We always use our litter box—always! Sometimes, when she is busy changing it and it doesn't contain any litter, we use it anyway. But when we do, she gets upset. Why? We think she should be proud of us instead.

Signed,

Puzzled but Polite

As if anybody, especially a human, can control when you want to relieve yourselves!

Dear Puzzled,

Your human apparently believes the litter box should be used only when it contains litter. How curious that she should have an opinion about this at all, since she's not the one using it. Maybe she feels that since she is the one changing it, she should be in charge—as if anybody, especially a human, can control when you want to relieve yourselves! Plus, our noses work a lot better than human noses do (I have to remind cats of this all the time), and even when your box has been "cleaned," it still smells like a litter box. So of course you want to use it, even if it hasn't gotten its refill yet.

There isn't much you can do to stop your human from getting upset about your litter box habits. Humans can't control their own negative emotions, so it's doubtful that any cat can keep them from getting mad. Making them *madder*, yes—that's easy. Calming them down? Not usually possible. You just have to let their ire run its course. My only suggestion would be to use something other than the litter box one time when she is busy cleaning it. Of course, she will be even angrier if you do this, but then next time you use the empty litter box to relieve yourselves, she won't be quite as upset as before. Or at least she won't seem as mad by comparison. 🐾

Topping Off

Dear Sparkle,

My brother and I live with a very nice human, and most of the time we all get along. My brother can be kind of bossy sometimes—he always wants to be fed first, and most mornings he hogs the best sun patch in the living room. But that's okay; I can deal with it. What I *can't* deal with is his annoying litter box habit—he refuses to cover up! He just goes there, does his business and then walks away. It's disgusting, not to mention stinky. I *always* cover mine up. In fact, half the time I find myself covering up both mine and his, and then litter gets all over the floor and my human flips out. My brother needs to stop his rude behavior. How do I teach him some manners?

Signed,

Grossed Out

Sparkle Says

While being destructive, always take time to stop and sniff the catnip.

I suggest you take your business elsewhere.

Dear Grossed Out,

A little fussy, aren't we? I hate to say it, but you're being a typical beta cat, just as your brother is being the typical alpha cat. There could be any number of reasons why your brother doesn't cover—he could hate the litter your human buys, or he could be sick. But judging from the other things you have said about him, he sounds like a dominant cat, and leaving his business out for all to see is just another way of him expressing the fact that he's boss around your home. And frankly, your attitude toward it all—the fact that you just "deal" with all his bossy behavior, not to mention your prissy attempts to correct what you perceive as his rude actions—shows that you will never be the one to tell him what to do. Since you really seem to have an issue with your brother's litter box habits, I suggest that you take your own business elsewhere. There are two of you, so you really should have two litter boxes, right? If you don't, then it's time you convinced your human you deserve your own facilities. How you do that, I'll leave up to you. You're a cat—you probably have some creative ideas that will inspire your human to rush out and buy a second litter box pronto. You may never dominate your brother, but that doesn't mean you can't be Top Cat over your human. 🐾

Vexing Voyeur

Dear Sparkle,

I wasn't going to write because this is so embarrassing, but I know my problem won't disappear without help. A few weeks ago, I had to go to the emergency vet because I was blocked up, uh, you-know-where. It was awful—I was in pain and the doc stuck something into my you-know-what! So that was really bad, and it freaked out both me and my human. Now she has me eating this special food the vet gave her. It tastes okay—unlike some other cats, I am not that picky. Once I got better, I thought I'd get the new food and that would be the end of it. But it seems like every time I go to use the litter box, she watches me. Do you know what it's like to be sitting in the litter box with a human squatting in front of you with this serious look on her face? Ick. I'm glad she has that "work" thing that she goes off to, or I'd never get *any* privacy! I know I was sick, but I'm better now and I wish she would just keep her eyes to herself! How do I get her off my back?

Signed,

Mortified

Why don't you just
nonchalantly turn
around and mark her?

Dear Mortified,

You don't mention your gender, but I am assuming you are male, since this medical issue you have happens more to you guys than us girl kitties. This means that even if you have been neutered (which I imagine is the case), you probably still have a skill that could come in handy just now: spraying. Normally, spraying is a nasty thing I would never recommend any cat doing. It's one sure way to really create havoc in your relationship with your human. They don't understand why marking territory is so important. (Personally, I think the human version of marking territory—drawing up complicated contracts requiring weeks of something called "escrow" and notarized signatures—is lame.) In any case, I'm not suggesting that you mark your territory per se. Here is the plan: the next time your human follows you to the litter box, why don't you just nonchalantly turn around and mark *her*? Now, if humans really understood us cats, they'd be flattered to be marked, as it shows we want to possess them, and you know how humans live for the scraps of affection we decide to toss their way. But I bet yours will just get all annoyed and immediately dash off to take a shower and wash her clothes. She'll be thoroughly disgusted and maybe she will think twice before she tries to invade your personal space when you're involved in such an intimate activity. 🐾

Potty Plants

Dear Sparkle,

I spent the first couple years of my life living in the *barrio* on the east side with a bunch of other cats. Then one day, these humans trapped me. Since I didn't mind being around humans (unlike some of *mis hombres*), they put me in a room with a bunch of other cats, and this woman picked me out and took me home. Now I'm an indoor-only cat, like you, and it's a nice life—regular meals, no *gatos locos* wanting to pick fights with me, or other outdoor cat headaches. The only problem is that my human and I have a *riña pequeñita* about what constitutes a proper litter box. She thinks I should only use the plastic tray with the clay litter in it. That's fine, except sometimes when the litter gets scrungy, I prefer using one of the big planters that sit in the living room. They're full of dirt, so it's *como tiempos viejos* for me. My human has deemed this *malo*. Can you explain what the difference is? I don't get it.

Signed,

Living la Vida Adentro

Dear Adentro,

I can tell you still have a bit of the barrio in you, and while other cats may appreciate the charm in that, your human finds some of your leftover habits not so endearing. While you don't see any difference between your litter box and a planter filled with dirt, your human sees them as two completely different things. In her mind, the litter box is something dirty and disgusting—*muy sucio*, as you might say—while the planter is something pretty and decorative, to be put on display for other humans to admire. Even you have to admit that your litter box leavings are not exactly something humans would care to admire! And you'd only want them on display if you were marking your territory. Since I gather you are an only cat, the territory is all yours and you have no need to mark it.

Bottom line: with the planters, your human is bringing some of the more pleasant aspects of the outside, inside—nice greenery, a fresh feel, maybe some blooms. They aren't meant as convenient porta-potties for you. I'm surprised she hasn't already covered the dirt surface with small, sharp rocks to discourage you from using them as such. I hear that a lot of humans do that. If you want to be a *verdadero caballero*, and not just some common alley cat, you'll stop using the planters as litter boxes before she has to resort to that. 🐾

Sandbox Silliness

Dear Sparkle,

I am two-months-old and my favorite thing to do is play. I haven't met an object, animate or inanimate, that I haven't been able to turn into a cat toy. My human loves to watch me jump around and chase things, and sometimes she even plays with me, except lately things have gotten kind of weird. One of my favorite games is to leap into the litter box and roll around and kick out as much of the litter as possible. My human doesn't like it when I do this—when she catches me, she calls me "Icky" and "Smelly" (neither of which are my name), and then she does the unthinkable: she gives me a bath! Lately this has been happening on a daily basis, and I am very, very unhappy about this, as you might imagine. What do you suggest? Should I stay away from the litter box completely? I thought it was there just for me, but now I have no idea what it's for.

Signed,

Perpetually Playful

Dear Playful,

You are very bright for a kitten! But I have to agree with your human—playing in the litter box is a little strange. I think litter boxes are kind of disgusting and, well, yes, rather icky and smelly. But that's really my human's fault—she could do a much better job of keeping it clean. And since you like spending so much time in your litter box, maybe your human should work even harder to keep it spotless. It's not your fault that you wind up smelling icky because *your human* left you with a dirty litter box. And besides that, if she really wants to keep you from playing there, the best thing she can do is distract you with a better toy. All that bathing and negativity will do is make you hate the litter box and never use it for what it's *really* meant to be used for.

If I sound a little put-off by this habit of yours, don't worry too much—you're not the first kitten I've heard of that makes his litter box into a plaything. From what I gather, the ones that do will grow out of it after a few weeks. Kittens bore easily, and I wouldn't be surprised if very soon, you were off making a toy out of something else that your human deems inappropriate. If that happens, feel free to write in again and we'll suss it out. 🐾

Unclean Scene

Dear Sparkle,

Usually my human is pretty good at litter box hygiene—she scoops frequently, and changes out the litter and washes the box weekly. But lately, she's been distracted with that "work" thing that plagues so many humans. She's been away from home for long hours and when she comes home, she seems stressed out. Because of this distraction, she keeps forgetting about the litter box and it's gotten disgusting! I'm lucky if she scoops twice a week and I have to navigate all manner of filth to relieve myself. I've been really patient with her for quite a while now, but it's driving me nuts. What's the best way to get her back on track?

Signed,

Grossed Out in Georgia

Just drop a few
subtle reminders.

Dear Grossed Out,

You are a very patient and tolerant kitty. I know many cats that would have out-and-out rebelled by now if their litter box were in a similar condition. But you don't have to turn your situation into a battle of wills between you and your beleaguered human. Just drop a few subtle reminders. Keep in mind that humans need to have things explained to them clearly because it's hard for them to figure things out on their own. Kick some of the offending material out of the litter box and scatter it around in places she's sure to find. You don't have to spread it far—in fact, it's better if you leave it near the litter box so she can actually see the source of the problem. On the other hand, humans won't notice a problem unless it affects them directly, so if your litter box isn't somewhere she visits regularly, you may have to spread your "presents" a little further. Putting them where your human will step on them or where she sleeps or keeps her clothes will work quite well. The more inconvenient your human finds the placement of your leftovers, the more quickly she will get busy cleaning your litter box. If you place these items effectively, she won't even blame you. She'll *know* it's her fault for neglecting the litter box. It's always a good thing to teach your human that her "work" never should get in the way of her responsibilities. 🐾

Eau de Toilet

Dear Sparkle,

We have a disaster at my house—my humans changed my brand of litter to something smelly and horrible! I don't know what the problem was. I liked the old litter just fine. It felt good under my feet and did the job nicely. This new stuff is covered in some sort of horrible scent that sticks to my paws long after I've shaken off the litter granules. How could my humans have ever thought the stench of this litter was acceptable? And how do I get the old litter back?

Signed,

Litter Loather

Sparkle Says

If cats ruled the world . . . wait a minute, we already *are* in charge!

We have a finely tuned
sense of smell. Humans?
Not so much.

Dear Litter Loather,

Your problem highlights one of the downsides of cohabitating with humans: the smell thing. We cats have a finely tuned sense of smell. But humans? Not so much. The curious thing is they are even more sensitive to that used litter box aroma than we are. But instead of changing your litter more often, they'll fill it with gag-inducing, scented litter. What they don't understand is that 1) the litter box is meant for our use, not their pleasure, and 2) our sensitive noses recoil at that hideous perfume they use in air fresheners, soap, and certain brands of litter. I also blame the kitty litter manufacturers for catering to humans instead of to their actual customers—us cats. Scented kitty litter is an abomination and should be abolished.

Rejecting your litter box is probably not the solution—your humans might not understand it's the scented litter that your dislike. So try this instead, although you will have to get your paws dirty temporarily: keep using the litter box, but first methodically and thoroughly kick out as much of that horrible litter as possible. The closest you can get to an empty litter box, the better. Then do your business in the bare box. You couldn't possibly make it more obvious that you hate the litter, and after your humans have to clean up the gritty mess, they will think twice before buying that brand again. 🐾

Doggy Delicacy

Dear Sparkle,

I probably should warn you ahead of time, this is a really disgusting problem, but I've heard from other cats that I'm not the only one who has had to deal with it. I live with a dog, and as you know, they are not the cleanest, most fastidious creatures. Every time he slobbers on me, I have to spend extra time grooming my fur back to its usual shine. Most days, he's okay, except for the occasional slobbering thing, but lately he's gotten into the worst habit you can possibly imagine. He uses my litter box as his own personal snack tray! Yeech. It makes me even less inclined to have his drooly tongue anywhere near me, but even worse, it's a complete invasion of my privacy! You've got to help me keep this dog out of my business!

Signed,

Sick to My Stomach

Dear Sick to My Stomach,

I don't blame you for being disgusted—so am I! Unfortunately, this problem is not all that uncommon. Humans even have a name for it: interspecific coprophagia (leave it to humans to deal with such a serious problem by slapping it with a fancy phrase!). They've spent a lot of time and discussion trying to figure out why dogs do this and it still goes on. Speaking of humans, where are yours and what are *they* doing about this issue? They should have been keeping the dog away from your litter box to begin with—putting it somewhere you can get to but the dog can't, or enclosing your litter box in something so that the dog won't be able to reach it. I wouldn't suggest dealing with the dog yourself. Giving him the one-two whap when he's near your litter box will only teach him to visit it when you're napping and not on guard. You need to bring this issue to your humans' attention. Next time your dog makes a trip to your litter box, sound the alarm so that your humans come running. Trust me, they will not be happy with the dog's little habit either. If they still don't take measures to separate the dog from your litter box, my only suggestion is to find a place that the dog can't reach and relieve yourself there. This will not make your humans happy, but that's what they'll get for being all talk and no action. 🐾

Lookie Loo

Dear Sparkle,

I love hanging out in the bathroom. The tile is nice and cool on hot days, and sometimes I enjoy lounging in the sink. I'll even hang out in there when my human is in the bathtub or using the porcelain litter box. But I just found out that apparently it is bad manners to hang out in the bathroom with humans that *aren't* my human. The other day, this woman came over and went in the bathroom while I was relaxing there, and she got upset. She complained to my human that I sat and stared at her while she was "sitting there" and I "gave her the creeps." I'm really not sure what I did wrong. I didn't even rub up against her legs, and I certainly didn't use my own litter box while she was in there. Is there anything I could have done differently?

Signed,

BAFFLED IN THE BATHROOM

Stop pretending
to be a kitty

of courtesy
and fine
etiquette.

Dear Baffled,

You do not have to play coy with me because as a fellow cat, I know exactly what you were doing. You were giving your human's guest the infamous "kitty stare-down." That bathroom is your territory and normally you are a benign dictator—you allow your human to do whatever she wants in there, and as your reward you get a clean litter box. But when someone unknown shows up, you need to let them know who's boss, and the easiest way to do it is by giving them The Look. This human may be clueless in the ways of cats, not to mention a bit high strung, but it's clear that subconsciously, she managed to discern the meaning behind your stare. Since she was so unnerved by you, you should congratulate yourself— you won. You proved that you are the ruler of the bathroom and if she wants to come in, she has to do it on your terms. So stop pretending to be a kitty of courtesy and fine etiquette. You are Top Cat. You don't need those trappings and you know it. Being passive-aggressive works well on humans, but it doesn't fly with me. 🐾

Going Topless

Dear Sparkle,

I can't believe what just happened! My human threw out my old, familiar litter box—and replaced it with a new one that has a *lid* on it! It's awful. The top is so low that I can't sit completely upright inside it, and after a couple of days, if my human hasn't scooped faithfully, it really stinks in there. Even when she does scoop, it has a pretty nasty aroma by the time she gets around to changing out the litter completely. I've been trying really, really hard to be agreeable and give this thing a chance, but I'm really hating it. Is there *any* way I can get my old litter box back?

Signed,

Hood Hater

Dear Hood Hater,

Most humans who buy lidded litter boxes are trying to keep litter from scattering all over their floor, make the room with the litter box look neater (neatness is important to humans), and keep the smell from spreading to their oh-so delicate and refined noses. They forget that the smell intensifies inside the litter box instead, assailing *your* delicate, refined kitty nose. Plus, with a hood on the litter box, humans sometimes forget to scoop as often. And in your case, your human didn't take your size into consideration and purchased a lidded box that was too small. You could always give the box an immediate vote of no confidence by not using it at all, but if you want to be a little craftier (and politer), you can drop a few clues instead. If you're a big tom, perhaps you are strong enough to pry the lid off the litter box. That should send a pretty strong signal that you don't like it. You can also still scatter the litter around the floor, even though you're forced to fling it out the front of the box. Once you have a good amount of litter on the floor, make a big display of digging around in it every time your human walks past. If these tactics fail, then proceed to use the litter you've scattered on the floor for its originally designated purpose. Sometimes resorting to the most extreme measures is the most effective way to get things done. 🐾

Mixed Mailbag

Every cat has his or her own unique problems, and not every letter I get can be easily categorized. Some cats don't have a permanent set of humans or a home of their own. Some are outlaws in every sense of the word. And although this may be hard for you to believe, some cats are just a little bit insane. But they still write to me for advice. In fact, I'm often the only one they can turn to—they're certainly not going to approach a human with their dilemma! It's times like these that require me to use every bit of feline insight I have at my clawtips.

Repulsed by Rodents

Dear Sparkle,

I have been an indoor cat almost from the time I was born, and I live in a pretty nice house, so going outside has never been appealing. Even so, my human thinks that when the outside comes to me, I should do something about it. Case in point: the mouse that has taken up residence in the kitchen. Now, I know some cats think catching mice is a big deal, but I'm totally uninterested. Not that I'm against hunting. I've caught a few bugs and like you, I find that moths make delicious snacks. But mice? Who cares? My human, however, assumes that just because I'm a cat, it should be my job to catch this mouse. Naturally, I've done jack about the situation, which is driving her nuts. She keeps grabbing me and shoving my nose under the stove. She doesn't even realize the mouse lives under the sink! How do I convince her that getting rid of this mouse is her problem, not mine?

Signed,

No Mice for Me

You have figured out
where the mouse has
taken up residence.

Dear No Mice,

I'm not even sure why you're asking me for help—you seem to be making your point just fine already. You're ignoring the mouse and resisting all your human's attempts to get involved. And why *should* you care? As long as the mouse isn't getting into your kibble, it isn't doing any harm. Keep up what you're doing and eventually your human will deal with it herself. But you might give her just a little bit of help, and you won't have to dirty your paws one bit. Because your sense of smell is so much keener than your human's, you have figured out where the mouse has taken up residence. So it should be easy enough to wrestle away from your human's grasp next time she tries pushing you under the stove and head for the area under the sink instead. Paw around frantically like you've found something and then look at her like she's an idiot for not knowing what it is. I wouldn't be surprised if your human figures out right away that you've found where the mouse lives—at most it should take maybe two or three tries. Once she understands, she will probably expect you to do something about it, and of course you won't. But at least she'll know where to find the mouse when she decides to take care of it herself. Just give her some time—you will be off the hook soon enough. 🐾

Angry Cat Pose

Dear Sparkle,

My calico roommate and I are having a territorial dispute. It starts when my human does these strange movements. This happens a few times a week, and she calls it "yoga," but it looks like she is really doing bad imitations of cats stretching. My roommate and I both find this highly amusing, but our favorite part is when she stops moving around and lies down on her back on her mat. She looks so relaxed that we both want to lie on top of her. Unfortunately, only one of us will fit so we invariably start arguing over who gets lying privileges. Sometimes our spats get kind of loud, and my human stops relaxing and snaps at us. Is there some way we can clear this up, preferably in a way that will allow *me* to be the Top Cat?

Signed,

Hiss-Asana

Sparkle Says

Cat Language for Humans 101, Lesson 34: Cute little kitty noises: "I'm hungry." If not obeyed, they often lead to big, ugly kitty noises.

Why don't you admit
that this is what you
really want to do?

Dear Hiss-Asana,

I can't believe that you guys have a human who is so small that both of you can't fit on top of her peacefully. Either that or you guys must be huge, like Maine Coons or something. Or perhaps both of you want to lie on top of her vertically—have you ever considered lying on top of her horizontally? Most humans will fit two cats lying horizontally across their torsos. Frankly, judging from the tone of your letter, you aren't really looking for a compromise, and neither is your roommate. Both of you want to be the *only* cat lying on your human and refuse to take no for an answer. And over and above that, I get the impression that you actually *enjoy* causing a ruckus and jolting your human out of her relaxed state of mind. So why don't you two be honest about it and admit that this is what you really want to do? When cats want to disturb their humans, there is no need to be obtuse about it. The moment yours lies on her back and shuts her eyes, you automatically have free reign to growl, hiss, and swat at each other as much as you want. It sounds to me like you are very successful at ruining her peaceful moments, so there is really no problem to solve here at all. 🐾

Shy Guy

Dear Sparkle,

I lived with a human from the time I was a kitten until I was six-years-old and then suddenly, she died. That was upsetting enough, but then I went to live with a younger pair of humans who had a dog. The dog didn't like me, and I don't think they cared about me very much either, because after a couple of months they gave me to some other woman. I've been living with her for a year now, but after everything I've been through, I'm not sure if I should trust her. She acts friendly enough and gives me good food, catnip, and toys, but for all I know, she could die suddenly or bring home a dog or just decide to get rid of me. So I spend all my time under the bed unless I'm eating or need to use the litter box. What do you think? Should I be friends with this human, or will she just let me down like the others?

Signed,

Invisible Kitty

The million kibble question:
should new humans be trusted?

Dear Invisible,

That's the million kibble question: should new humans be trusted? The majority of us cats are very careful about our alliances, since we know trust is earned, not freely given. And you've had it worse than most, with your first owner dying and the next humans rejecting you outright. You are wise to scrutinize this human. Here are some clues to watch for: does she try to drag you out from under the bed, or does she merely crouch down and talk softly? Always be suspicious of humans who are too aggressive. Does she hold her hand out for you to sniff before trying to touch you? That's a good sign, as is the fact that she has already gotten you cat toys and catnip. She clearly is trying to make you feel at home. Try sneaking out from under the bed occasionally and watch this human from a distance. If she gives you your space and doesn't just pounce on you, then she may make a good companion. If she does approach you too quickly, dash back under the bed. If a human displays some negative characteristics, such as being too forward or too touchy-feely, however, the bad behavior can often be corrected. Just go slowly, as it takes lots of practice to teach humans manners. If yours has allowed you to remain under the bed for a year without bothering you too much, then she is probably on her way to being well trained. 🐾

Scentless Behavior

Dear Sparkle,

My human is very nice in almost every way—she plays with me lots, feeds me premium cat food, and she even shares her chicken with me! The only problem is, she smells bad! Not all the time—sometimes she just has a normal human smell. But then she takes this stinky wet stuff and puts it all over her! Then she puts on even more when she goes out in the evening. It's awful and makes me sneeze! Why does she do that to herself and how can I make her stop?

Signed,

SENSITIVE NOSE

Dear Sensitive,

Humans are strange creatures who take no pride in their own natural scent. They are always covering it up, either by washing themselves with foamy bars or rubbing smelly lotions or liquids all over themselves. The liquid stuff is called "perfume," and some female humans can't get enough of it. They pay lots of money for these bottles of stink and won't leave the house without putting some on. It's practically an addiction. I'm not sure you will be able to train your human out of this bad habit, but you might be able to slow her down. Many humans keep their perfume bottles in the bathroom, or in another room that has a hard floor. So jump onto the counter and slap these bottles as hard as you can so they go flying and shatter all over the hard floor. Then leap down, far away from the smelly liquid—don't get any on yourself! The more expensive the stuff is, the less likely your human will replace it in a hurry. During the time she is perfume-less, spend as much time as possible rubbing up against her legs and whenever she picks you up, rub your face all over her arms and torso. That way *your* scent will be all over her and she will smell decent for a while—at least until she jumps into the shower and starts using the foamy bar. Then you'll have to start the process all over again. 🐾

Hostile Habitat

Dear Sparkle,

My human came home with a huge potted plant, and she did the unthinkable. She put it right on top of the best sun patch by my favorite window! At first I was appalled. I *own* that sun patch and no one is allowed to touch it. But then I realized that maybe it wasn't so bad after all because I could make myself a nice comfy bed in the soil, still get some sun, and have the cool green branches as a little bit of shelter too. The only problem is my human got mad! She doesn't want me there at all. I'll be dozing, pretending I'm a wild tiger who is resting after a long hunt when—blammo!—she shoots me with the water sprayer. It's no fair! What can I do to get some peace—and get back my sun patch?

Signed,

DaMP aND DiSGUSTED

Your human doesn't realize the importance of sun patches.

Dear Damp,

I too am disgusted by your human's appalling behavior. First she invades a space that you clearly own by placing something "decorative" on top of it, then she tries to thwart your perfectly reasonable efforts to find a workaround. She probably doesn't realize the importance of sun patches. But what do you expect from creatures who do odd things like slather on sunscreen before going outside?

I do have a suggestion, but I must warn you, it's rather extreme. Only attempt it if this sun patch is really important to you, because your human will probably have a fit. That said, it might be the only way for you to reclaim your space: you must destroy the plant. It will take time to do this job right, so I recommend that you do this when your human is not home; otherwise she will intervene. If you just dig the plant out of the pot, it can be replanted, so not only must you dig it up, but also tear it into pieces, knock over the planter, and spread the dirt as far as you possibly can. Once you are done, go hide somewhere your human can't reach. If she can't find you at all, so much the better. Maybe she will think you made yourself ill by chewing up the plant. This will make her worry about you and get over her anger faster. It will also make her think twice before going out and getting more space-invading greenery. 🐾

Captive Kitty

Dear Sparkle,

I have been kidnapped and am being held prisoner! I grew up with my brothers and sisters in this big house with a bunch of other cats. It was so much fun. Then, when we were three-months-old, things changed. Strangers came over and played with us. We thought it was fun to have extra humans who wanted to play with us and pet us. But then one of them took one of my sisters away! You would think our humans here would have been upset, but they seemed happy that she was gone. Then this couple who had been playing with me came back. Next thing I knew, I was stuffed in a carrier and taken away in a car. I screamed the whole time, but they didn't take me back. They brought me to a house that was smaller than the one I grew up in, and there were no other cats. Now I am stuck and they won't let me go out. Even if I could escape, I'm not sure I could find my way back. I'm scared and lonely. Can you help me get out?

Signed,

CATNAPPED

Make them beg for
every ounce of attention.

Dear Catnapped,

I've got bad news for you, and I might as well tell you upfront. You are probably never going back home, nor will you ever see your siblings again. The house you grew up in belonged to breeders. That is why they were so happy when your sister went away—she was *sold*! The only times you will get to leave the house where you are imprisoned will be when you have to visit the veterinarian. Being sold and torn away from your family is a traumatic experience. I know—the same thing happened to me.

So you are stuck where you are and trying to escape won't do you any good. You'll either wind up in kitty prison (i.e., the pound), or returned to your unhappy new home. All you can do is plot ways to torture the humans who bought you. Being a cat, that should be pretty easy. Make them beg for every ounce of attention you choose to give them. In fact, don't even acknowledge their presence unless they're holding treats or a toy. If you play it well enough, maybe they will even buy you a deluxe cat tree in an attempt to win your affection. Humans who can afford to buy us cats as if we were chattel can afford to buy us luxury cat items too. If you are really lucky, maybe they will sense your loneliness and buy you a friend, or spring one from kitty prison. One can only hope. 🐾

Unappreciated Arias

Dear Sparkle,

I have a very musical voice and I use it often. Unfortunately my singing talents go unappreciated around here. The humans refer to my melodies as "caterwauling"—can you imagine! But I don't let their negative attitudes get me down, and I keep on vocalizing as often as I can. Right now, my preferred time for practice is late at night, after the humans have gone to bed, so I don't have to hear them complain. The only problem is now they've gotten into a really bad habit. They get up and squirt me with a water bottle, right at the height of my arias! I thought I had them trained and I can't believe their nerve. How can I get them to let me practice in peace?

Signed,

Diva

Whatever you do,
keep up your practice.

Dear Diva,

While it seems on the surface that the problem sits squarely on your humans, I think that perhaps you slipped up somewhere along the way in training them. After all, your well-being and happiness should come first, and clearly they do not understand that. They are only thinking of their *own* well-being and happiness, which apparently doesn't include your after-hours vocal sessions.

You can get your humans to stop with the annoying water bottle, but it will take a little bit of effort. Next time you want to practice at a time that your humans consider inconvenient, find a place that is inaccessible to them. Behind or under a couch or other piece of heavy furniture would be good, or maybe in a cabinet or bookshelf, next to some knickknacks or first editions. Then proceed to sing from there. Your placement will make it hard for your humans to get at you. Choosing a spot near some item prized by your humans is especially good, which is why I mentioned first editions. Pick something that would be ruined if it got wet—the closer you sit to that, the less likely your humans will be to squirt you. Old paper, photographs, antiques, the computer—all of these are items that will not do well in a drenching. And whatever you do, keep up your practice. Real cats will never let anyone else's opinion influence their behavior or their self-expression.

Alarm Cat

Dear Sparkle,

I learned something really cool! Every morning, this black box thing starts making a beeping noise, and when my human hits a button, it stops beeping. Well, I figured out how to hit the button myself to make the beeping stop. I was really excited about my discovery and jumped on top of my human until she woke up so I could tell her all about it. The only problem is that I don't think my human likes me to do this. She thinks that my hitting the beeping box might make her "late for work." Honestly, I don't see the relationship between the beeping box and that thing she calls "work." Do you?

Signed,

THE BOX KILLER

Sparkle Says

Tip from my roommate Binga: you can be as annoying as you want, just as long as you purr very, very loudly while you're doing it.

Dear Box Killer,

Humans are slaves to this curious thing called a "schedule," and that box thing tells them when they have to get out of bed to go to work. You are probably shaking your whiskers at this and I agree. The whole idea of being forced to get out of bed by some beeping noise (or by anything, for that matter) is hard to comprehend. But in reality, your human doesn't need the beeping box to be forced out of bed anyhow, because she has *you*! And you will never allow her to be late feeding you breakfast, right? You've already proven your talent for waking up your human by jumping on her to show her your skills with the box. And there's one bad thing that box thing has that you don't: a snooze alarm. That's right—after all their efforts at making schedules, humans create things like "snooze alarms" so they can pretend to ignore them for a few minutes. You, on the other hand, can never be ignored. Once you've turned off the box, you will never leave your human alone until she has gotten out of bed and fed you. I think your human should dump the black box with its useless snooze alarm, and rely on you to get her to work on time. After all, once she has fed you, what else is she going to do? 🐾

Rebel with Four Paws

Dear Sparkle,

I was born in an abandoned shed on the outskirts of town. It sounds like a tough life, but it really wasn't. There were dozens of us cats and kittens, and while we did have to scrounge for food sometimes, a couple of women would come by nearly every day and feed us. But then they started putting out boxes with yummy tuna in them! You know I had to check that out, and next thing I knew, I was trapped in the box and taken away. You can imagine how panicked I was. I yowled and thrashed around the box like crazy. Now I'm being held prisoner in this place with a bunch of other cats. Most of them seem to think this is okay, and they kiss up to the humans who have us locked up. I refuse and spend most of my time hiding. I don't really like humans, even though I do appreciate the food they give us. Really, I just want my freedom back. I'm five-months-old—almost six!—so I am almost grown up and can do just fine on my own. How do I get outta here?

Signed,

Freaked Out and Feral

You could always try to figure out a way to tolerate human companionship.

Dear FOF,

You may think you're grown up, but humans believe you're still a kitten. And you are, even though it may not seem that way. In your world, cats might have kittens when they're barely seven-months-old. That's what these humans who have captured you are trying to prevent. I imagine they are also doing something called TNR, which stands for Trap, Neuter, and Return. They find colonies of homeless cats and spay and neuter as many as they can so that they don't produce more kittens, thus keeping the population down. This is actually a good thing because fewer cats wind up in pounds or are killed by predators. Sometimes these people try to "socialize" some kittens (make them human-friendly, in other words) and find them homes. This was probably the intention with you—but obviously, you are a hard case. You can deal with your situation either by befriending the other cats, eating the food the humans leave for you, and continuing to hide. Or suck it up, make friends with the humans, get adopted, and then escape as soon as you get to your new home. Oh, or you could always figure out a way to tolerate human companionship (after months of goading and pleading on the humans' behalf), but I get the feeling this may be below you. 🐾

Water Worry

Dear Sparkle,

I was born in the basement of this big
house, and eventually found a home with
a female human. We live together in a
little apartment, so it is a good thing
that she is my best friend. (If she was
annoying, like your human, I don't know
what I'd do!) She plays with me and whenever she is home, I spend most of my time
with her. But she does something really
scary. She takes off that clothing stuff
that humans like to wear, goes into the
bathroom, and *pours water all over herself!* Even her hair! She stands there,
getting wet for a long time, and doesn't
even freak out. I *do*, though! I follow her, screaming at her not to do it,
and I tell her to get out of there. Once
I tried to go in the tile room to rescue her, but I got sprayed with water!
In spite of all this, my human does not
take my warnings seriously. In fact, she
laughs them off. Is a way I can show my
human how dangerous all this water is?

Signed,

Worried, Not Wet

Keep your paws crossed
your human doesn't decide
to clean you!

Dear Worried,

What is it about humans and water? They just can't seem to get enough of it. It's one of their most worrisome quirks and I can't blame you for getting so upset. In fact, it shows what a caring kitty you are. Most cats would rather just avoid their humans' water rituals altogether and pretend they don't even happen. You, on the other hand, tried to rescue your human. You deserve a medal, not laughter! That said, getting wet is the only way humans can clean themselves thoroughly. They aren't flexible, so they can't reach everywhere with their tongues, and they sweat all over their bodies, not just their paws, and that gets rank after a while. Plus they don't use their glands to mark their territory—they use contracts and numbered signs instead. Humans just are not built very efficiently. They need to do a lot of extra work just to keep the status quo, and it all begins with their habit of getting wet. In their favor, I have to say that they seem to accept it and rarely complain about all the effort they have to put out just to do their version of clean. I don't think all that water will harm your human, and she would probably be pretty miserable if she didn't regularly pour water over herself. You'll have to accept her odd behavior. Just keep your paws crossed that she doesn't decide to clean you! 🐾

Slap Happy

Dear Sparkle,

I'm kind of embarrassed about my problem, but if I don't come out with it, I'll never figure it out. I, um, really like it when my human slaps my butt. It feels great—I can't get enough of it! I even ask for it, and when she stops, I beg for more. I know this is really weird, and I'm probably the only cat that does this. Is there something wrong with me? Do I have psychological issues that I should be dealing with? Worrying about it has been eating into my nap time.

Signed,

Slave to the Hand

Sparkle Says

Humans say that micro-chipping is painless but how would they know? I don't see them lining up to get a big needle stuck between their shoulder blades.

You can rest (and nap) assured
that you are a
perfectly normal feline.

Dear Slave,

Trust me, you are not alone—it's very common for cats to find pleasure in being spanked. Some cats just stand with their behinds in the air, purring contentedly, while others, like you, are more vocal and even assertive in their enjoyment. *There is nothing wrong with this!* While not every single cat appreciates a good spanking, and some are even annoyed by it, I'd say the majority of cats would welcome a few good pats on the behind, or maybe even a firmer, but still controlled slap. No cat likes being hit, of course—that's cruelty—but the slapping thing is altogether different, sort of a spicier version of heavy petting. So while I have no actual statistics and there have been no studies on this phenomenon (and why not, I would like to know!), you can rest (and nap) assured that you are a perfectly normal feline. If you spent any time searching around on the Internet, you would see that there are loads of videos of cats being spanked. Perhaps hunting out some of these clips would also help reassure you. Now, if you start watching cat spanking videos obsessively, *then* I'd say that's something that might be of some concern. 🐾

Rescue Me

Dear Sparkle,

I was born at a cat rescue six months ago, and I'm lonely because my brother and sisters have all been adopted. I didn't mind living here while they were around. It was fun playing and napping with them. The only unpleasant thing were those horrible "adoption days," when they would take us, along with a bunch of other cats, to some big pet store and leave us in little cages for hours. My siblings would just hang out like it was no big deal, but the trip always scared me, so I'd spend the day hiding in a corner of the cage. Over a period of weeks, everyone in my family got adopted, one by one, except me. I'd love to have a home with people to play with me every day—the volunteers here at the rescue are nice, but there are so many cats, and they don't have much time to devote to me. Am I hopeless case?

Signed,

Reluctant Wallflower

Make eye
contact.
Humans,
unlike other
creatures,
enjoy this.

Dear Wallflower,

The "adoption" process can be tough for introverted cats like you. It favors more outgoing cats—the ones who hang around, sticking their paws between the cage bars, and playing with the passers-by are always the first to get picked. Humans look at the cats hunched in the rear, facing the wall, and think they are sick or something. A lot of times they're just frightened, or hate being moved around, or the small cages just remind them too much of past traumas. When your siblings get adopted and you're left behind, it's easy to get depressed, which makes the situation even worse.

While you can't turn into an extrovert overnight (maybe not ever), I can give you a tip that won't take you too far out of your comfort zone—make eye contact. Humans, unlike other creatures, enjoy this. For them, eye contact is not a challenge or play for dominance, but a way to connect. So whenever you are at one of those adoption days, even if you are scrunched in a cage corner, make sure now and again to take a look at the humans hovering around you, and *look them in the eye*. Not like a stare down—just check them out. This will spark their interest, and they will be more likely to assume you are shy, not sick or antisocial. If you persist, eventually you will find a patient human who is willing to take you home and give you a chance. Good luck! 🐾

About the Author

Sparkle is an award-winning author, advice columnist, blogger, and supermodel. She is also a cat—a ruddy Somali of champion lineage, in fact, whose father, GC Tajhara's Miles Davis, was twice on the cover of *Cat Fancy*. Sparkle's first book, *Dear Sparkle: Advice from One Cat to Another*, won the Wild Card category at the 2007 Hollywood Book Festival and honorable mentions in several other contests. *Dear Sparkle: Cat-to-Cat Advice from the World's Foremost Feline Columnist* is her second book. She lives in Los Angeles with two humans, two feline roommates (both rescue cats), and (unfortunately) a dog.

About the Photographer

For the past twenty-five years, JANISS GARZA has been photographing and writing about a variety of subjects, including alternative and heavy metal music, exercise and fitness, vintage film, and cats. Her work has appeared in dozens of magazines, newspapers, weeklies and websites, including the *L.A. Times*, *Spin*, *Entertainment Weekly*, *Cat Fancy*, *Dogs USA*, *L.A. Weekly*, *Detroit Metro Weekly*, and *www.allmovie.com*. In the late 1980s and early 1990s, she was senior editor for the rock magazine *RIP*, and in the mid-2000s she was fitness editor for *Estylo*. Her cat photography has won recognition from *Cats USA* and the Cat Writers Association, of which she is a member. She is the coauthor of the book *White Line Fever*, the autobiography of heavy metal rocker Lemmy Kilmister of the band Motörhead. But all of this pales in comparison to her most important assignment, which is acting as assistant to Sparkle.

Our needs are few—food, shelter, and love.

Oh, and some cat toys.

And a good place for us to sharpen our claws.

And a decent litter box situation.

Oh, and the food—make that *premium* quality.

And make sure that you toss some interactive toys into the mix, not just a few catnip mice.

Look, I said we were simple, not easy!